Five Star Films

Elizabeth A. Mejia

&

Frederick O'Connor

Washington State University

Library of Congress Cataloging-in-Publication Data

Mejia, Elizabeth A., 1958–
     Five star films/Elizabeth A. Mejia & Frederick O'Connor.
          p.   cm.

     ISBN 0-13-035536-4
     1. English language–Textbooks for foreign speakers. 2. Motion
pictures–Problems, exercises, etc. 3. Readers–Motion pictures.
I. O'Connor, Frederick H. II. Title. III. Title: 5 star films
PE1128.M378 1994   93-44648
428.2–dc20   CIP

Director of Production and Manufacturing: *David Riccardi*
Electronic Production Coordinator: *Molly Pike Riccardi*
Creative Director: *Paula Maylahn*
Acquisitions Editor: *Nancy Baxer*
Electronic Production/Design Manager: *Dominick Mosco*
Electronic production/supervision and interior design: *Steve Jorgensen*
Page Composition: *Steve Jorgensen*
Electronic Art: *Freddy Flake*
Cover Design: *Merle Krumper*
Production Coordinator: *Ray Keating*

©1994 by Prentice Hall Regents
Prentice-Hall, Inc.
A Paramount Communications Company
Englewood Cliffs, NJ 07632

Printed in the United States of America

10   9   8   7   6   5   4   3   2   1

ISBN   0-13-035536-4

Prentice-Hall International (UK) Limited, London
Prentice-Hall of Australia Pty. Limited, Sydney
Prentice-Hall Canada Inc., Toronto
Prentice-Hall Hispanoamericana, S.A., Mexico
Prentice-Hall of India Private Limited, New Delhi
Prentice-Hall of Japan, Inc., Tokyo
Simon & Schuster Asia Pte. Ltd., Singapore
Editora Prentice-Hall do Brasil, Ltda., Rio de Janeiro

Printed on Recycled Paper

Contents

Acknowledgments

The authors would like to thank the following people:

Kevin Costner and Lynn Whiteford of TIG Productions for their gracious permission to use materials from *Dances with Wolves.*

Kathy Lendech of Turner Entertainment for her enthusiastic assistance with permission for *Casablanca* and *Gone with the Wind.*

Paul Arcario for his insightful review of the manuscript.

Nancy Baxer for shepherding this project to completion.

Steve Jorgensen for his able work in design and layout.

In addition, Liz Mejia would like to thank:

her parents, Tom and Miki Kennedy

her daughter, Pamela

G.D.

Rick O'Connor would like to thank:

Masumi, Tim, Mike, and Harrison

Duke and Libbie

About This Book

Five Star Films is an intermediate-level, content-based, listening-speaking book designed for use with classes of mature ESL students.

This book is predicated on a few basic beliefs about language learning, especially about learning spoken English:

1. The best language instructional materials are those that use authentic samples of speech. This is true even for very low-level materials.

2. Language is a multidimensional experience. The visual impression of film is important to complete the learner's experience with language.

3. Comprehension of discourse requires the learner to actively attempt to achieve closure between points of comprehension. In other words, a good learner takes those points that he or she understands and attempts to "close the gap" between them by means of guessing.

4. Language learning is a "sense"ual experience. It is a communication act between a teacher and a learner. Like all sensual acts, it should be pleasurable. Language learning should be fun, both for the student and the teacher.

How This Book Is Structured

Authentic text taken from one of five different American movies forms the core of each chapter in this book. The goal of each chapter is to prepare students to watch the complete movie highlighted in the chapter.

Each chapter develops six critical scenes from the movie. A critical scene is a scene of one to three minutes that is critical to establishing the narrative, character development, or tone of the movie.

Each scene is developed by several speaking and listening activities. These activities all serve one goal: to assist students in whatever way possible to further their comprehension of the scene and its relationship to the other scenes in the movie.

At the end of the scene activities, the students watch the movie. Pre-viewing questions and post-viewing discussion questions and follow-up activities are given for each movie.

Suggestions are made for other movies that the student might find enjoyable.

The fundamental premise of this book is simple and in direct contrast to most listening-speaking books: All language activities are structured to help students understand discourse.

How to Use This Book

For purposes of schema-building, we suggest that you use this book sequentially. *Gone with the Wind*, the first movie in this book, has a Civil War theme that should help students in watching the next movie, *Dances with Wolves*. The racial and civil war theme carries over into *To Kill a Mockingbird*. *Casablanca* sets the schema for *When Harry Met Sally*.

This is not a "teacher-proof" book. It is not the kind of book that can be picked up and put into use on short notice. To use a film, any film, well, one must be prepared. A teacher should have watched the entire film at least once, and preferably several times, before attempting to use it.

While we have attempted to explain directions as carefully as possible, only careful pre-class review of the activities can ensure successful use of this book. To assist in locating scenes from the films, scripts have been included in the Appendix beginning on page 137.

The authors of this book would like to emphasize that they support only the legal use of movies for educational purposes. The Copyright Law of the United States limits the ways that movies can be used, even in educational settings, but there are a number of useful alternatives available to teachers and students. The authors would like to encourage all persons using this book to investigate the legal ways to show movies in educational settings.

This book is dedicated to the cause of the
Native American. We urge you to join us in
the support of Futures For Children,
Albuquerque, New Mexico.

Chapter 1

Library of Congress

As You Begin

Directions:

Read the following short passage. Look at the picture. Then, in groups of three or four, discuss the questions.

Each country has events in its history that stand out as turning points. In most countries, however, there is one event that has had a greater effect than all others. In a sense, this event defines the country. It may be a revolution, a war, an invasion, or any other similar event. This event serves as a foundation by which the actions, options, and dangers of today are analyzed.

1. What event in your country's history was the most significant? What made it so important?

2. What single events in other countries you know about were the most important for the people of those countries?

3. What event do you think was the most important for the United States? Why do you think it was so important?

A Reading to Get Things Started

Directions:

Read the following passage. Use your dictionary to find words that you don't know. After you have finished reading, discuss the answers to the questions with a classmate or a small group of your classmates. Read the vocabulary list before you begin.

Vocabulary List

State's Rights - The political rights of individual states within the United States.

the Federal Government - The national government of the entire United States. The headquarters are in Washington, D.C.

Abraham Lincoln - The president of the United States during the Civil War.

Robert E. Lee - The most important general of the Confederate army, the army of the Southern states during the Civil War.

the cabinet - A group of advisors to the president of the United States.

Except by Violence

The Civil War is probably the most significant single experience in our national existence. It was certainly the biggest tragedy in American history and, at the same time, probably did more to shape our future than any other event.

It settled two things once and for all. In the first place, it determined that there would be one nation, and not two or more, between Canada and Mexico; that there would be unity in the American Republic, that the old theory of **State's Rights** would wither to the extent that the **Federal Government** would have the power and the authority to enforce an overall national policy for the entire country.

In addition, the war ended the institution of chattel slavery. That was an institution that the country could not have carried into the twentieth century without suffering a crippling handicap. It is not easy to see how the institution could have been disposed of, except by violence. It had imbedded itself too deeply, not only in the Southern economy and by indirection in the Northern economy as well, but in human emotions.

The existence of chattel slavery made it unnecessary for people to face up to the race problem. Once slavery was destroyed, and the Civil War did destroy it, the nation was left with a piece of unfinished business. It had political unity; it had to move ahead and create a moral and emotional unity as well. Freedom is something for everybody. There could no longer be grades and distinctions in American citizenship.

As it happened, **Abraham Lincoln** did not live to see the war end. He did know about **Lee's** surrender, and he knew, of course, that the war would very soon be over. He did not, however, see it end.

On the morning of April 14, Lincoln had a **cabinet** meeting in the White House. Everybody was feeling relaxed because Lee had surrendered, and Lincoln remarked that they were going to get big news somehow in the next twenty-four hours. His cabinet members wanted to know what made him think so. He said he had had a dream. It was a recurrent dream that he had frequently during the war, and every time he had it, it foreshadowed some great event—a huge battle, a big victory, a political move of some kind. Well, of course, people wanted to know what the dream was like, and Lincoln said it was rather mysterious. In the dream, he was on some sort of boat, moving rapidly forward over a dim, hazy sea toward, as he put it, a dark and indefinite shore. In the dream, he had never actually reached the shore, but when he woke up, he knew that big news, a big development of some kind, was about to take place.

He was quite right. That night, he went to Ford's Theater, and less than twenty-four hours after he told about his dreams, he was dead. He had, presumably, reached that dark, indefinite shore. He left his country with the war won, moving likewise on a mysterious vessel across a mysterious sea, toward a dark, indefinite shore. There was no chart for that shore, because nobody had ever been there. We still don't have a chart, but we are still on our way. We are crossing the seas on which the Civil War put us afloat. Like Lincoln, we are moving toward a destiny bigger than we can understand. The dark, indefinite shore is still ahead of us. Maybe we will get there some day if we live up to what the great men of our past won for us. And when we get there, it is fair to suppose that instead of being dark and indefinite, that unknown continent will be lit with sunlight.

From *Reflections on the Civil War* by Bruce Catton. Copyright © 1981 by Gerald Dickler as the executor of the estate of Bruce Catton and John Leckley. Used by permission of Doubleday, a division of Bantam Doubleday Dell Publishing Group, Inc.

Questions for Discussion

1. What two major questions did the Civil War settle?

2. Once slavery had been ended, what problem remained to be solved?

3. When Lincoln had his recurrent dream, what did it usually signal?

4. What was the great event that was signalled by his dream on April 13?

5. What does the author mean when he says that "[the] country with the war won, [was] moving likewise on a mysterious vessel across a mysterious sea"? What is that sea?

6. What does the "dark and indefinite shore" symbolize?

7. Why are there no charts for that shore?

8. What does "sunlight" represent in the last sentence of this piece?

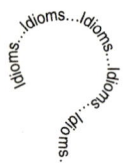

Idioms from the Film, *Gone with the Wind*

Activity 1

Directions to the teacher:

Read the following list of idioms and have students repeat them for correct pronunciation.

Directions to the students:

Listen as your teacher reads the following list of idioms. Pay attention to the teacher's pronunciation. Then study the list. These idioms are from the video scenes you will be working with.

---

1. to be up to (something) ↔ to be doing (something)

Definition: to be doing something, especially to be doing something possibly naughty or unexpected

Example: I don't know what he*'s up to.*

Example from the film: What *are* you *up to?*

Language note: The question "What are you up to?" is also used as an informal greeting meaning "How are you?" The normal response is, "Nothing" or "Nothing much."

---

2. to care about (someone) ◆→ to love (someone)
Definition: to love someone, either in a platonic or romantic sense
Example: She really *cares about him.*
Example from the film: And I know you must *care about me.*

3. to lead (someone) on ◆→ to deceive (someone) [especially in romance]
Definition: to deceive someone, particularly to fool someone into thinking that you care about him/her
Example: She doesn't care about him. She's just *leading him on.*
Example from the film: You *led me on*!

4. to take advantage of (someone) ◆→ to mistreat (someone)
Definition: to abuse someone, particularly someone who has shown you a kindness
Example: He *took advantage of* his teacher's kindness.
Example from the film: First you *take* a low common *advantage of me*—then you insult me!

5. to strike someone as ◆→ to seem to be
Definition: to seem to be a certain way, particularly on first acquaintance
Example: She *strikes me as* a trustworthy person.
Example from the film: He doesn't *strike me as* half good enough for a girl of your—what was it?—"your passion for living?"

6. to fix things ◆→ to be decisive
Definition: to be decisive, particularly to determine who will win in a conflict situation
Example: This match should *fix things* as to who the better player is.
Example from the film: There's a little battle going on right now that ought *to* pretty well *fix things* one way or the other.

Language note: Another meaning of this idiom is to repair things or relationships.

---

7. one way or the other ◆→ either positively or negatively
Definition: either in one direction or the other, particularly in conflicts or decisions
Example: I can't make up my mind *one way or the other.*
Example from the film: There's a little battle going on right now that ought to pretty well fix things *one way or the other.*

8. to come down around (one's) ears ◆→ to fall apart
Definition: to fall apart, to disintegrate
Example: If we don't get that contract, I can see this company *coming down around our ears.*
Example from the film: No use staying and letting the South *come down around your ears.*

9. white trash ◆→ low-class white people
Definition: low-class white people, particularly in the southern United States
Example: Those people are nothing but *white trash*.
Example from the film: Well Miss Ellen she went down to nurse that Emmie
Slattery, that *white trash*, and she took down with it too
and last night she…

Language note: This is a very insulting term.

---

10. to be tipsy ◆→ to be slightly drunk
Definition: to be slightly drunk
Example: I shouldn't have any more wine. I *'m* a little *tipsy* already.
Example from the film: You'll make yourself *tipsy*.

Language note: This idiom is somewhat outdated.

Activity 2
Directions to the teacher:

Have students read the following sentences. Instruct them to try to rewrite the sentences, replacing the items in bold print with one of the idioms from the list in Activity 1.

Directions to the students:
Read the following sentences. Then rewrite the sentences, replacing the items in bold text with idioms from Activity 1.

1. I'm afraid our relationship is **falling apart**. I don't know if he really loves me. I wish he would tell me **if he does or if he doesn't**.

   _____

   _____

   _____

2. I don't know what **he's doing**. He doesn't **seem to be** the kind of person who would **deceive** a friend.

   _____

   _____

   _____

Activity 3

Directions to the teacher:

Have the students work in pairs to complete the following dialogues using at least one idiom from Activity 1. After you have checked their work, have them practice the dialogues with their partners.

Directions to the students:

Work with a partner to complete the following dialogues. Be sure to use at least one idiom from Activity 1 in each dialogue. After your teacher has checked your work, practice your dialogue with your partner.

1. Situation: Two friends, Sally and Karen, are talking about Sally's boyfriend, Bob.

   Sally: I'm just not sure about Bob. I'd like to trust him, but I'm not sure if I can.

   Karen: _____

             _____

2. Situation: James and Pat are discussing plans for their upcoming vacation. Sally: I'm just not sure about Bob. I'd like to trust him, but I'm not sure if I can.

   James: It's a tough choice. On one hand, Yellowstone seems like the ideal vacation spot, but on the other hand, I'd like to see the coast.

   Pat: _____

             _____

3. Situation: Frank and Diane are discussing their boss, whom neither of them likes.

   Diane: I can't believe he'd do something like that. I mean, he can't just take our vacation time away whenever he feels like it, can he?

   Frank: _____

             _____

4. Situation: Madeline and Katrina are talking about someone they have just interviewed for a job in their company.

   Madeline: I explained to her that there would be a lot of overtime and that it would be important to be pleasant with the customers even when we're really busy.

   Katrina: _____

             _____

5. Situation: Betty and Jim are talking about the new neighbors who just moved in last week.

   Betty: Can you believe it? They just throw their garbage out on the front lawn. And those rusty old cars they have parked all over the place. It's disgraceful.

   Jim: _____

             _____

Scene 1 In the Library at Twelve Oaks

Movieland Wax Museum

Idioms in this scene

> to be up to (something)
>
> to care about (someone)
>
> to lead (someone) on
>
> to take advantage of (someone)
>
> to strike (someone) as

Activity 1

Directions to teacher:

> *Divide the students into pairs of A and B. Follow these directions for a silent narration: Have student A face the video screen. Have student B sit next to student A, but facing away from the video screen. Play the entire clip with the sound off.*

Directions to student A:

You are going to watch a scene from the movie *Gone with the Wind*. As you watch the scene, you will tell your partner (student B) what is going on in the movie. Student B will not be able to see the movie and neither you nor student B will be able to hear the movie. Keep these important questions in mind as you are telling your partner the story:

1. Who are the people in the scene?
2. Where are the people?
3. When does the scene take place?
4. What are the people doing?
5. What do you think they are talking about?

It's important to speak clearly and to think about the grammar and vocabulary you will use. Before you begin watching, think about these questions:

1. What tense(s) should you use to describe actions that are happening as you are describing them?
2. How will you refer to people? For example, if there are two men, how will you refer to them so that your partner understands which one you are speaking about?

Directions to student B:

You are going to be told about a movie. You will not see the movie. Your partner (student A) will tell you about the movie. Pay close attention. Try to listen for information to answer the following questions:

1. Who are the people in the scene?
2. Where are the people?
3. When does the scene take place?
4. What are the people doing?
5. What are they talking about?

Directions to the A and B students:

After partner A has described the scene to partner B, get together and discuss the scene. If partner B doesn't understand something about the scene, he/she should ask partner A to explain it again. A good question to ask, if you are not sure you understood something, is:

Would you mind repeating the part about ——? I'm not sure I understood it.

Then, watch the scene together one more time with the sound off.

Activity 2

Directions to the teacher:

Divide the students into groups of three or four. This is a speaking activity and does not require the video.

Directions to the students:

Get into groups of three or four. Use an English-English dictionary to look up these four words: *lady, woman, man, gentleman.* After you have looked up these words, discuss the answers to the following questions:

What is the difference between a lady and a woman?

What is the difference between a man and a gentleman?

Does your culture distinguish between ladies and women, between men and gentlemen? If so, how?

Activity 3

Directions to the teacher:

Play the entire scene twice with the sound on. Divide the students into groups of three or four to discuss the answers to the following questions. Review the answers in a large group discussion.

Directions to the students:

You will see and hear this scene two times. After you watch, discuss the answers to the following questions in groups of three or four.

1. Why does the woman think the dark-haired man is not a gentleman?
2. Why does the dark-haired man think the woman is not a lady?
3. What is the blond-haired man's name?
4. What is the woman's name?
5. What is the name of the woman whom the blond-haired man will marry?

Teaching Point

There are many types of questions in English. Many questions are simple questions. The speaker expects an answer. These are examples of **simple questions:**

Do you like chocolate? (The speaker expects to hear yes or no.)

What time is it? (The speaker expects to hear a time given.)

Complex questions are different. Sometimes the speaker does not expect to hear an answer. This type of question is a **rhetorical question.** Many times, the speaker supplies the answer.

> **Example: (In a university lecture) So what were the causes of the Civil War? Well, there were at least three important ones that historians generally mention.**

Sometimes the speaker asks a question that indicates that he/she is expecting a certain answer or wishes to communicate a certain feeling to the listener. These types of questions are called **biased questions**. There are many ways that a speaker can form biased questions:

- with tag questions and intonation

  You have heard about the Civil War, haven't you?

  (Speaker assumes the listener will say "yes.")

  You have heard about the Civil War, haven't you?

  (Speaker is a bit surprised and expects a "yes" answer.)

- with a supplied answer and rising intonation

  What do you want, my book?

  (Speaker could be a little angry and expecting a "no" answer, or the speaker could be expecting a "yes" answer.)

- with negative questions

  Didn't you study the Civil War in high school?

  (The speaker expects to hear a "yes" answer.)

Activity 4

Directions to the teacher:

Place the students in pairs. Show the entire scene twice with the sound on. Check for comprehension in a large group discussion.

Directions to the students:

In pairs, listen to the entire scene two more times. On your second listening, listen for the following questions. After you hear the question, write the following code after the question:

S • Simple question

R • Rhetorical question

B • Biased question

If you write B, make a note about what answer you think the speaker expects to hear. Share your answers with each other.

Who're you hiding from in here?

What are you up to?

Well, why aren't you upstairs resting with the other girls?

What is this Scarlett, a secret?

Well, isn't it enough that you've gathered every other man's heart today?

Have I your heart my darling?

Oh you do care, don't you?

Oh can't we go away and forget we ever said these things?

But how can we do that?

Don't you, don't you want to marry me?

Oh my dear, why must you make me say things that will hurt you?

How can I make you understand?

How could I help loving you?

Why don't you say it, you coward?

Who are you to tell me I mustn't?

Has the war started?

In the middle of that beautiful love scene?

That wouldn't have been very tactful, would it?

...what was it?

Activity 5

Directions to the teacher:

Show the scene one more time with the sound on. Then, divide the students in groups of three or four and have them discuss the answers to the following questions. Check for comprehension in a large group discussion.

Directions to the students:

In groups of three or four, listen to the scene one more time and discuss the answers to the following questions.

1. When did this scene take place? (Give as precise an answer as possible.)
2. What do you think will happen to these people?

Scene 2 At the Confederate Ball

Activity 1

Directions to the teacher:

Divide the students into groups of three or four. This is a speaking activity and does not require the video.

Directions to the students:

Look up the idiom *in mourning* in an English-English dictionary. In groups of three or four, discuss the answers to the following questions.

1. What do people in your country do when they are in mourning?
2. Do they wear special clothes?
3. Do they behave in a certain way?
4. How long does the mourning period last?

Activity 2

Directions to the teacher:

Group the students in pairs or triads. Show the clip one time for each group of questions. There are four groups of questions, so you will show the clip a total of four times. Have the students compare their answers after each listening. Review in a large group format.

Directions to the students:

With the members of your group, listen for the answers to the following questions. After the first viewing, answer the first question; after the second viewing, the second question; the third viewing, the third question; the fourth viewing, the fourth question. Discuss your answers with your group members after each viewing.

First viewing questions: What is Scarlett's full name?

What is the man's name?

Second viewing question: What is the other woman's name?

Third viewing questions: Who has Scarlett married?

Who has the other woman married?

Fourth viewing questions: For whom do you think these women are in mourning?

How do you know?

What did women in the South do when they were in mourning?

Activity 3

Directions to the teacher:

Give the following assignment for homework. Have the students research the topic and then share what they have learned with the class.

Directions to the students:

Prepare the following homework assignment and share the information with others in your class. Trace the history of the word *Yankee*. Explain how it is used within the United States and outside the United States.

Teaching point

Sometimes it is possible to figure out the meaning of a word from what is said about the word. For example, if you did not know the meaning of the word *anesthesiologist* you could figure it out from the following passage:

Woman: Well, my anesthesiologist gave me such a wonderful drug that I hardly felt any pain at all when I had my child.

What does an anesthesiologist do? What is an anesthesiologist?

Activity 4

Directions to the teacher:

Play only the clip of Dr. Meade's speech two times. Pair the students. Have them discuss the answers to the questions and then check for comprehension in a large group discussion.

Directions to the students:

Look up the words *blockade* and *schooner* in an English-English dictionary. Listen to the following clip from the scene two times. Listen for the term *blockade runner*. Answer the following questions. Discuss your answers with your partner.

What is a blockade runner?

Who is a blockade runner?

Why do you think there is a blockade?

Teaching Point

     Sarcasm is a way of expressing a feeling about something by saying the opposite. Sarcasm is often expressed by slow, clear speech in which the speaker emphasizes the words that say the opposite. Consider the following example:

     John hates dogs. He visits his sister, who has a dog.

     John: Would you mind putting the dog in the bathroom while I'm here? You know I LOVE dogs.

Activity 5

Directions to the teacher:

    Group the students in pairs or triads. Play the entire clip one time with the sound on. Check the answers in a large group review.

Directions to the students:

    In groups of two or three, listen to the clip and discuss the answers to the following questions. Concentrate on the last line that the man says.

        Draw a circle around the words the man emphasizes in the sentence:

    "And you, Mrs. Hamilton. I know just how much that means to you."

        What does the man mean when he says:

    "And you, Mrs. Hamilton. I know just how much that means to you"?

Scene 3 In the Parlor at Aunt Pittypat's

Idioms in this scene:

    to fix things

    one way or the other

Activity 1 (Clip 3A)

Directions to the teacher:

    This is a roundel activity. Separate the students into groups of four. Assign each student a number. Student number 1 must listen for the answer to question 1; student 2 for question 2; etc. Play the scene one time with the sound on from the beginning of the scene where Scarlett says, "Oh, oh, oh, what a darling thing" to where Rhett says "I always get paid." After they listen, have the student discuss the answers. Then, play the clip again so that the students can check the answers.

Directions to the students:

    You will be assigned a number. Listen to the clip one time. Find the answer to the question with the same number. Then, share the answer with the members of your group.

    1. Where has Rhett Butler been recently?

    2. What will he bring Scarlett next time?

    3. What information does Scarlett want from Rhett?

    4. What reasons does Rhett Butler give for bringing Scarlett gifts?

Activity 2
Directions to the students:

Look up the following words in your English-English dictionary. Then, in pairs, write and perform short dialogues in which you use these words.

flatter yourself

cheer up

last longer

Activity 3 (Clip 3B)

Directions to the teacher:

This is a roundel activity. Separate the students into groups of four. Assign each student a number. Student number 1 must listen for the answer to question 1; student 2 for question 2; etc. Play the scene one time with the sound on from the point where Scarlett says, "If you think I'll marry you just to pay for the bonnet, I won't" to the place where Rhett says "…the war can't last much longer." After they listen, have the student discuss the answers. Then, play the clip again so that the students can check the answers.

Directions to the students:

You will be assigned a number. Listen to the clip one time. Find the answer to the question with the same number. Then, share the answer with the members of your group.

1. What payment does Scarlett think Rhett wants?
2. What payment does Rhett want?
3. According to Rhett, why does Scarlett let him visit her?
4. According to Rhett, what is going to happen to the war?

Activity 4
Directions to the students:

For homework, find the answer to the following question about American history. You may want to look in a library or ask an American.

What happened at the Battle of Gettysburg? Try to find answers to the following questions:

Who fought in the battle?

Where was the battle fought?

When was the battle fought?

What was the result of the battle?

What famous event happened after the battle?

Directions to the teacher:

Have the students present the information they learned about the Battle of Gettysburg in short oral reports to the class before they watch clip 3C. Then, synthesize the information so that all the students have it.

Activity 5 (Clip 3C)

Directions to the teacher:

This is a roundel activity. Divide the students in groups of four. Assign each student a number. Student number 1 must listen for the answer to question 1; student 2 for question 2; etc. Play the scene once with the sound on from the beginning of the scene where Scarlett says, "Really, Rhett, why?" to where Rhett says "Some little town in Pennsylvania called Gettysburg!" After this, have the student discuss the answers within their groups. Then, play the clip again so that the students can check the answers.

Directions to the students:

You will be assigned a number and will listen to the clip one time. Find the answer to the question with the same number. Then, share the answer with the members of your group.

1. What information does Scarlett want to know about the war?

2. What information does Rhett give her about the war?

3. What information does Scarlett want to know about Ashley?

4. What information does Rhett give her about Ashley?

Activity 6

Directions to the teacher:

Play the entire scene one more time. Have the students get into groups of four to discuss the answers to the following questions.

Directions to the students:

Discuss the answers to the following questions after you view the scene.

1. What kind of person is Scarlett? What is she like? Do you like her? If so, why? If not, why not?

2. What kind of person is Rhett Butler? What is he like? Do you like him? If so, why? If not, why not?

Scene 4 In Rhett's Buggy in the Streets of Atlanta

Idiom in this scene:

to come down around (one's) ears

Activity 1

Directions to the teacher:

Divide the students into groups of three or four.

Directions to the students:

In groups of three or four, look up the following words in your English-English dictionary and answer the following questions.

panic

calling card

pay a visit

1. What's the connection between a "calling card" and "pay a visit"?

2. Do people in your country use calling cards? If so, in what circumstances do they use them?

3. Does the idea of "panic" fit with the ideas of "calling card" and "pay a visit"?

Activity 2

Directions to the teacher:

Assign pairs of students to research the following topic. Then, have the students do oral presentations. Have the entire class synthesize what they have learned.

Directions to the students:

Work with another student to find out information about the life of General William T. Sherman. Present your information to the other students in your class.

Activity 3 (Clip 4A)

Directions to the teacher:

Group the students in pairs. Play the first part of the scene from the beginning where Rhett says, "Scarlett! Scarlett! Whoa! Whoa! Climb into this buggy" through the point where Scarlett says "Don't talk to me like that, Rhett. I'm so scared. I wish I could get out of here." Have the students work in pairs on the answers to the questions and then play clip 4A again. Review the answers in a large group discussion.

Directions to the students:

Watch the beginning of this scene and fill in the missing dialogue below. Then discuss the answers to the questions.

Rhett: Scarlett! Scarlett! Whoa! Whoa! Climb into this buggy. This is no day for walking. You'll get run over.

Scarlett: Oh Rhett, Rhett, drive me to Aunt Pitty's please.

Rhett: _____?
Whoa. That's just another of General Sherman's calling cards. He'll be paying us a visit soon.

Scarlett: I gotta get out of here. I gotta get out of here before the Yankees come.

Rhett: _____?
Or have you had enough of death and lice and men chopped up? Well I suppose you weren't meant for sick men, Scarlett.

Scarlett: Don't talk to me like that, Rhett. I'm so scared. I wish I could get out of here.

1. What kinds of questions are these? Simple, rhetorical, biased?

2. What is General Sherman's calling card?

Activity 4

Directions to the teacher:

Play all of Scene 4 with the sound on. Divide the students into small groups of three or four. Have students focus on the lines written below.

Directions to the students:

In small groups, watch this scene and focus on the way the actors say the following lines. Discuss the answers to the questions below.

Panic's a pretty sight, isn't it?

Well I suppose you weren't meant for sick men, Scarlett.

Don't talk to me like that, Rhett.

A man who understands you and admires you for just what you are.

Answer the following questions:

1. What's different about the way Rhett talks and the way Scarlett talks?

2. What is strange about the way Rhett uses the words *pretty, understands,* and *admires?* Think about what you have already learned in Scene 2. What word do we use to describe this type of speech?

3. When Scarlett says, "Don't talk to me like that," what does "like that" mean?

Activity 5

Directions to the teacher:

Play the last two lines of the scene several times. Divide students into As and Bs. Have the As write Scarlett's line and the Bs write Rhett's line.

Directions to the students:

Watch the short clip from the scene that your teacher will play for you. If you are an A, write down all of Scarlett's words. If you are a B write down all of Rhett's words.

Scarlett: _____

_____

_____

Rhett: _____

_____

_____

Now compare your work with another student's. If you are an A, compare your work with another A. If you are a B, compare your work with another B. After you have finished comparing your work, discuss your answers to the following questions.

1. Does Scarlett really hate Rhett?

2. Will she hate him until she dies?

3. What does Rhett mean by "not that long"?

4. What are Rhett's feelings for Scarlett at the end of this scene?

Scene 5 In Aunt Pitty's House and the Flight from Atlanta

Activity 1

Directions to the teacher:

Show the first part of the scene (from the point where Rhett and Scarlett enter Melanie's bedroom through the point where someone throws a chair through a shop window) with the sound off. Follow these directions for a silent narration:

Have student A sit facing the video screen.

Have student B student sit next to student A student facing away from the video screen.

Play the entire clip with the sound off.

When the students have finished working in pairs, show the same part of the scene with the sound on, letting both students see the screen.

Directions to student A:

You are going to watch a scene from the movie *Gone with the Wind*. As you watch the scene, you will tell your partner (student B) what is going on in the movie. Student B will not be able to see the movie and neither you nor student B will be able to hear the movie. Keep these important questions in mind as you are telling your B partner the story:

1. Who are the people in the scene?
2. Where are the people?
3. When does the scene take place?
4. What are the people doing?
5. What do you think they are talking about?

Directions to student B:

You are going to be told about a movie. You will not see the movie. Your partner (student A) will tell you about the movie. Pay close attention. Try to listen for information to answer the following questions:

1. Who are the people in the scene?
2. Where are the people?
3. When does the scene take place?
4. What are the people doing?
5. What are they talking about?

Directions to the A and B students:

After partner A has described the scene to partner B, get together and discuss the scene. If partner B doesn't understand something about the scene, he/she should ask partner A to explain it again. When you finish talking, each of you should write a paragraph about the scene. Write the paragraphs without consulting each other. When you have finished, read each other's paragraphs and discuss any differences or omissions. Now watch the scene again with the sound on.

Activity 2

Directions to the teacher:

Show the second part of the scene (from the point where the men see the buggy and start chasing it to the point where the flaming building collapses) with the sound off. Have the students change position within the same pairs so that those who were As become Bs and visa versa. When the students have finished working in pairs, show the same part of the scene with the sound on, letting both students see the screen.

Directions to student A:

You are going to watch a scene from the movie *Gone with the Wind*. As you watch the scene you will tell your partner (student B) what is going on in the movie. Student B will not be able to see the movie and neither you nor student B will be able to hear the movie. Keep these important questions in mind as you are telling your B partner the story:

1. Who are the people in the scene?
2. Where are the people?
3. When does the scene take place?
4. What are the people doing?
5. What do you think they are talking about?

Directions to student B:

You are going to be told about a movie. You will not see the movie. Your partner (student A) will tell you about the movie. Pay close attention. Try to listen for information to answer the following questions:

1. Who are the people in the scene?
2. Where are the people?
3. When does the scene take place?
4. What are the people doing?
5. What are they talking about?

Directions to the A and B students:

After partner A has described the scene to partner B, get together and discuss the scene. If partner B doesn't understand something about the scene, he/she should ask partner A to explain it again. When you finish talking, each of you should write a paragraph about the scene. Write the paragraphs without consulting each other. When you have finished, read each other's paragraphs and discuss any differences or omissions. Now watch the scene again with the sound on.

Activity 3

Directions to the teacher:

Show the entire scene to the whole class with the sound on and ask the students to answer the questions in small groups.

Directions to the students:

Watch the entire scene one more time. Before you watch the scene, read the following questions. After you have watched the scene, discuss the questions in small groups.

1) Where are they going?

2) Why are they leaving Atlanta?

3) Why are the men able to try to steal their horse? Are the men soldiers?

Scene 6   Return to Tara

Idioms in this scene

white trash

to be tipsy

Teaching Point

    There are many different ways to **divide a scene** into sections. For example, you can divide a scene by place. You can divide a scene by focus. You can divide a scene by topic. You can divide a scene by subject.

Activity 1

Directions to the teacher:

Show the entire scene to the whole class with the sound on. Ask the students to give a name to each of four parts and write a few words describing each one.

Directions to the students:

Watch the scene with the sound on. On the left, give a name to the part of the scene based on the place where the scene happens. On the right, write a few words describing the basic topic of that part. Then go over your answers in small groups before discussing them with your teacher.

1. _____   _____

2. _____   _____

3. _____   _____

4. _____   _____

> **Teaching Point**
>
> **Emphasis** and **pitch** are two ways that speakers can show emotion in their speech. Generally, important words are emphasized. They seem to JUMP out of the sentence. In addition, the pitch with which they are spoken is somewhat louder and higher. For example, if two people are sitting in a baseball stadium, one might say to the other:
>
> Did you SEE THAT BALL? Wasn't that INCREDIBLE?

Activity 2 (Clip 6A)

Directions to the teacher:

Play the first part of the scene, with the sound on, through the point where Scarlett says "It's still there." Play it several times. Allow students to work in pairs between the viewings. Review the answers in a large group.

Directions to the students:

View the part of the scene your teacher will play for you. As you watch the scene, mark the emphasis and pitch of Scarlett's voice for the lines below. The first one has been done for you.

      •   •   •

Melly, we're home! We're at Tara!   _____

I can't see the house. Is it there?   _____

I can't see the house. Have they burned it?   _____

It's all right! It's all right!   _____

They haven't burned it! It's still there!   _____

Discuss your answers with your classmates and your teacher. Now go back and write down a word that shows the emotion behind each line (for example, "sadness") in the blank to the right of the line.

Activity 3 (Clip 6B)

Directions to the teacher:

Play the second part of the scene with the sound on, from the point where Scarlett says, "Mother! Mother! I'm home" to the point where Pork says, "If there's anything I can do, Miss Scarlett." Then ask the students to answer the following questions in small groups. You may wish to play the scene more than once.

Directions to the students:

In small groups, view the second part of the scene as your teacher plays it for you. Then, answer the following questions.

1. What is Scarlett's mood at the beginning of the scene?

2. What is Scarlett's mood at the middle of the scene?

3. What is Scarlett's mood at the end of the scene?

Teaching point

Often, speakers use **intonation,** the rising and falling "music" of the voice, to show emotion. Rising intonation often shows surprise, disbelief, and even fear. Falling intonation is often used to show finality or the "factualness" of something. Listen as your teacher models the following dialogue and discuss what the different intonations mean. You should also hear a change in the pitch level with which the words are pronounced.

A: Dinner? (Question: Do you want dinner?)

B: Dinner? (Disbelief: I can't believe you are suggesting dinner. I just ate an hour ago.)

A: Dinner. (Reiteration: That's right; you heard what I said. I asked if you wanted dinner.)

B: Dinner. (I am still dumbfounded.)

Activity 4 (Clip 6B)

Directions to the teacher:

Play the second part of the scene again, pausing after each of the lines written below. Discuss the meaning of the emphasis, pitch, and intonation of the lines with the students, and then have students mimic the intonation of the lines.

Directions to the students:

View the second part of the scene again. Listen for the lines written below. Your teacher will pause after each of the lines. Try to figure out what the pitch, emphasis, and intonation of the lines mean. Then, practice saying the lines yourselves using the same pitch, emphasis, and intonation.

1. Oh, oh Pa, I'm home. I'm home.

2. Oh, Mammy. I'm so, so...where's Mother?

3. But where's mother?

4. Mother, mother, mother, mother?

Activity 5 (Clip 6C)

Directions to the teacher:

Play the third part of the scene with the sound on, from the point where Scarlett says, "What'd you do with Miss Melly?" to the point where Pork says, "They took them the first day, and what'd they leave they carried off across their saddles." Divide the students into groups of three or four and have them do the exercise. Check for comprehension in a large group discussion.

Directions to the students:

In groups of three or four, listen to the third part of the scene. Do the exercise with your group and then share your answers with the other students in your class.

1. List the various things that the Yankees did to Tara.

2. List the problems that Scarlett must face in the rest of the movie.

Activity 6 (Clip 6D)

Directions to the teacher:

Play the fourth part of the scene, with the sound on, from the point where Scarlett says, "Don't tell me anymore about what they did" through the point where Scarlett says "Katie Scarlett's home. You needn't worry." Play it several times. Allow students to work in small groups between the viewings. Review the answers in a large group.

Directions to the students:

View the part of the scene your teacher will play for you. Between each viewing, work in pairs or small groups to answer the following questions.

1. What is wrong with Scarlett's father? What do you think has happened to him?

2. What is the problem with their money?

3. How has Scarlett matured since the first part of this scene? How does the scene show this?

4. What other problems can you add to the list you developed in the previous activity (Scene 6, Activity 5)?

Activity 7

Directions to the teacher:

Play the entire scene, with the sound on. Have students work in pairs after the viewing to answer the following questions. Review the answers in a large group discussion.

Directions to the students:

View the whole scene again. After your view it, work in pairs or small groups to answer the following questions.

1. What differences can you hear between Scarlett's language at the beginning and at the end of this scene?

2. Characterize Scarlett's attitude at the beginning of the scene and at the end of the scene. (What was Scarlett like at the beginning of the scene? What was she like at the end of the scene?)

3. What do you think the changes in Scarlett's language and attitude mean?

Pre-Viewing Questions

Directions:

Consider these questions as you watch the movie. Be prepared to discuss them after you have seen the movie.

1. *Gone with the Wind* has four distinct parts:

   1) before the war

   2) in Atlanta during the war

   3) at Tara after the war

   4) with Rhett after the war

   As you watch the film, identify one part that you most enjoyed watching. Be prepared to explain why you liked that part of the film.

2. What kind of film is *Gone with the Wind?* Is it a romance, a coming-of-age film (a film in which a character makes the transition from childhood to adulthood), or an historical film?

3. *Gone with the Wind* is a film about people under pressure. As you watch the film, think about how you might react under similar pressures.

4. *Gone with the Wind* is a film about the events in one woman's life and the changes those events cause. Try to identify some of the major events and some of the changes that they cause.

5. Scarlett O'Hara is one of the most popular heroines in American fiction. As you watch her personality develop on the screen, try to compare her to American women that you may know. What personality traits does she share with them? What personality traits are not shared?

Post-Viewing Questions

Directions:

After watching the film, discuss the answers to these questions in small groups.

1. Which part of the film did you most enjoy watching? Why?

2. Think about Scarlett's relationships with other women before her mother dies. Then think about Scarlett's relationships with other women after her mother's death. Is there any difference?

3. What do you think will happen to Scarlett after the end of the film?

4. Did you think that *Gone with the Wind* was a romance film, a coming-of-age film, an historical film, or some other kind of film? Explain the reasons for your opinion.

5. Thinking about the pressure that the characters in the film were under, how do you think you would behave under similar pressure?

6. Explain what you think were the most important events in the life of Scarlett O'Hara and the effect that they had on her.

7. Explain what you think, from your own experience, are typical characteristics of American women based on the model of Scarlett O'Hara. Explain how you think Scarlett might be different from other American women. What characteristics are similar to those of women in your country? Which are different?

Post-Viewing Activities

1. Pick one scene from the film, write out the dialogue, assign actors and perform the scene in class.

2. Read Chapter 1 of Margaret Mitchell's book *Gone with the Wind* and compare it with the opening scenes of the movie.

3. Have a discussion about the four major characters in the film. To get ready for the discussion, fill in the following chart.

   Check one box for each character. Give the reasons for your choice on the right.

I WOULD CHOOSE:		HUSBAND/WIFE	FRIEND	PARTNER	BECAUSE
Scarlett O'Hara					
Rhett Butler	as my				
Ashley Wilkes					
Melanie Wilkes					

If You Liked This Film

You may wish to see these other films about Southern women:

Jezebel (1938) starring Bette Davis and Henry Fonda. Directed by William Wyler (103 min. black and white).

A Street Car Named Desire (1951) starring Vivien Leigh and Marlon Brando. Directed by Elia Kazan (122 min. black and white).

Chapter 2

New Mexico State Tourist Bureau/Wyatt Davis

Courtesy of the American Museum of Natural History

Eugene Gordon

As You Begin

Directions:

Read the following short passage. Look at the pictures. Then, in groups of three or four, discuss the questions.

   Many countries have groups of indigenous people. Indigenous people are usually minorities and they are always the original people who lived in an area. African-Americans are an American minority, but they are not indigenous because they were not the first people to live in this land. Native Americans are a minority and they are indigenous because they were the first people to live here.

1. What are some countries in the world where indigenous people live? Can you name the groups of indigenous people who live in those countries?

2. What do you know about the culture and history of those indigenous people?

3. How do the governments of those countries treat the indigenous people?

A Reading to Get Things Started

Directions:

Read the following passage. Use your dictionary to find words that you don't know. After you have finished reading, discuss the answers to the questions with a classmate or a small group of your classmates.

The War for the Black Hills

After the American Civil War, rumors started that the Black Hills of South Dakota were filled with gold. These hills were the sacred mountains of the Sioux Indians and had been given to the Indians by treaty in 1868. However, the rumors of gold were so strong that white men soon forgot about the treaty and invaded the Black Hills, looking for gold. In 1874, the U.S. Army sent an expedition into the Black Hills, under the leadership of General George Armstrong Custer. Custer made the situation worse by announcing that the hills were filled with gold and soon even more white miners were ignoring the treaty and seeking gold in the hills. This invasion of their sacred land infuriated the Sioux, who rallied behind the leadership of two famous Indian leaders: Crazy Horse and Sitting Bull.

The Indians protested the violation of the treaty to the federal government in Washington and for a while the Army did try to stop the miners from entering the hills. Soon, however, the president of the United States sent out a commission "to treat with the Sioux Indians for the relinquishment of the Black Hills." Dee Brown, in his book *Bury My Heart at Wounded Knee*, tells what happened next:

> To ensure representation of all Indians, runners were sent to invite Sitting Bull, Crazy Horse, and other "wild" chiefs to the council. Sitting Bull told the messenger, "I want you to go and tell the President that I do not want to sell any land to the government." He picked up a pinch of dust and added: "Not even as much as this." Crazy Horse refused to attend the council.

> The commissioners recognized the futility of trying to buy the hills and decided instead to negotiate for the mineral rights.

> The chiefs debated very earnestly the question of the Black Hills. During three days of speech making, the chiefs made it quite clear to the President's representatives that the Black Hills could not be bought cheaply, if at any price. Spotted Tail, one of the chiefs, asked the commissioners to submit a definite proposal in writing.

> The offer was four hundred thousand dollars a year for the mineral rights; or if the Sioux wished to sell the hills outright the price would be six million dollars payable in fifteen annual installments. Spotted Tail rejected both offers firmly. The Black Hills were not for lease or for sale.

> The commissioners packed up, returned to Washington, reported their failure to persuade the Sioux to relinquish the Black Hills, and recommended that Congress disregard the wishes of the Indians and appropriate a sum fixed "as a fair equivalent of the value of the hills." This forced purchase of the Black Hills should be "presented to the Indians as a finality," they said.

> In this way a chain of actions was set in motion which would destroy forever the freedom of the northern Plains Indians.

Condensed and adapted from *The War for the Black Hills* from *Bury My Heart at Wounded Knee*. Reprinted by permission of Sterling Lord Literistic, Inc. Copyright © 1971 by Lee Brown.

Questions for Discussion

1. Why were the Black Hills important to the Sioux Indians?
2. Why were white people interested in the Black Hills?
3. Why did the Army originally go into the Black Hills?
4. How did the Indians feel about the white men coming to the Black Hills?
5. What was the purpose of the commission that the president sent to the Sioux?
6. What was the final offer that the U.S. government made for the Black Hills?
7. How did the Indians respond to the offer?
8. Read the last sentence carefully. What do you think happened to the Sioux and the Black Hills?

Idioms from the Film, *Dances with Wolves*

Activity 1

Directions to the teacher:

Read the following list of idioms and have students repeat them for correct pronunciation.

Directions to the students:

Listen as your teacher reads the following list of idioms. Pay attention to the teacher's pronunciation. Then study the list. These idioms are from the video scenes you will be working with.

1. to take cover ◆→ to get out of the way of danger
Definition: to get behind something so as not to be hit during a battle
Example: The soldiers *took cover* during the firefight.
Example from the film: You'd better *take cover*.

2. not to be kidding ◆→ to be serious
Definition: to emphasize that you are serious
Example: I'm *not kidding* when I say I'll quit.
Example from the film: I ai*n't kidding*.

3. to settle (something) ◆→ to come to a conclusion about (something)
Definition: to reach a conclusion about some matter
Example: We have to *settle* this disagreement before we can get anything done.
Example from the film: If we ain't gonna fight, we could just *settle this* whole business with a little high stakes poker.

4. to be posted ◆→ to be assigned to a military post
Definition: to be sent to a military post for duty
Example: He *was posted* to Fort Dix last summer.
Example from the film: Well it says here that you're *to be posted* on the frontier.

5. to never fail to (do something) ◆▸ to always (do something)

Definition: to be totally consistent in doing something

Example: He *never fails to* turn in his homework.

Example from the film: He still won't eat from my hand but his keen eyes and ears *never fail to* alert me when something is wrong.

6. bogey man ◆▸ a scary imaginary figure [especially used to frighten children]

Definition: a scary figure used to frighten people, especially children

Example: Go to sleep now. There's no *bogey man* to be afraid of.

Example from the film: They are not the *bogey men* they have been made out to be.

7. to be made out to be (something) ◆▸ to be characterized as (something)

Definition: to be characterized in a certain way, usually negatively

Example: Crime in this city is not as bad as it is *made out to be.*

Example from the film: They are not the bogey men they have been *made out to be.*

**8. to not be able to bring (oneself) ◆▸ to be unwilling or
    to (do something)   unable to (do something)**

Definition: to be unwilling or unable to do something because of one's own sense of what it right and wrong

Example: I could*n't bring myself to* tell her that I didn't like her new dress.

Example from the film: I sense that I made a mistake in doing so but I could *not bring myself to* take it back.

**9. To take (something) back   ◆▸ to withdraw (something)
    to take back (something)   which was said**

Definition: to withdraw a remark which you regret having made

Example: I *take back* what I said about your always being late.

Example from the film: I sense that I made a mistake in doing so but I could not bring myself to *take* it *back.*

10. to turn (something) ◆▸ to become (something)

Definition: to become something different than what you were

Example: You've *turned* conservative.

Example from the film: *Turned* Injun, didn't you, didn't you?

Language Note: This idiom is usually used negatively, as a criticism or accusation.

Activity 2

Directions to the teacher:

> *Have students read the following sentences. Instruct them to rewrite the sentences, replacing the items in bold print with one of the idioms from the list in Activity 1.*

Directions to the students:

Read the following sentences. Then rewrite the sentences, replacing the items in bold text with idioms from Activity 1.

1. I was very insulted when I heard him say that I had **become a coward**. I **have always** supported him when he was in trouble. I **won't even talk** to him unless he **withdraws** that remark.

   _____

   _____

   _____

2. I'm **completely serious** about this problem. We have to **solve** this problem right away. I don't think our competitors are **the monsters** that you say they are. I want you to stop **describing** them that way and find a creative solution to our problems.

   _____

   _____

   _____

Activity 3

Directions to the teacher:

> *Have the students work in pairs to complete the following dialogues using at least one idiom from Activity 1. After you have checked their work, have them practice the dialogues with their partners.*

Directions to the students:

Work with a partner to complete the following dialogues. Be sure to use at least one idiom from Activity 1 in each dialogue. After your teacher has checked your work, practice your dialogue with your partner.

1. Situation: Bill is telling Francis about one of his co-workers, Sam.

   Bill: I'm so angry with him! How dare he question my honesty. After all the help I've given him over the years, I just can't believe he'd say something like that!

   Francis: _____

              _____

2. Situation: Annie is a pilot in the Air Force. She has just received new orders. She's telling Neil, another officer, about them.

   Annie: Not Texas! I can't stand Texas again. It's so hot, and the base is miles and miles from town. I'm disgusted.

   Neil: _____

   _____

3. Situation: Tim is talking with his mother about a fight he had with his brother.

   Tim: It's not my fault. He started it. I know I shouldn't have called him a stupid liar, but I was so angry.

   Mother: _____

   _____

4. Situation: Carla is telling her friend Linda about her discussion with her husband about buying a house.

   Carla: Bill wants to buy it, but I'm not so sure. It's all we talk about any more. And the owners are pressuring us for an answer. We just don't seem to be able to make up our minds, and I just don't know what to do.

   Linda: _____

   _____

5. Situation: David is telling his friend Mark about the people at his new job.

   David: You wouldn't believe these people. All day long with never a smile. Everyone's so super-serious. I don't know how they stand going to work every day. And it's so quiet. It's like working in a library.

   Mark   _____

   _____

Scene 1 On the Battlefield

Idioms in this scene:

    to take cover

    not to be kidding

    to settle something

Photofest

Activity 1

Directions to teacher:

Divide the students into pairs of A and B. Follow these directions for a silent narration:
Have student A face the video screen. Have student B sit next to student A but
facing away from the video screen.
Play the entire scene with the sound off.

Directions to student A:

You are going to watch a scene from the movie *Dances with Wolves*. As
you watch the scene, you will tell your partner (student B) what is going on
in the movie. Student B will not be able to see the movie and neither you
nor student B will be able to hear the movie. Keep these important
questions in mind as you are telling your partner the story:

1. Who are the people in the scene?

2. Where are the people?

3. When does the scene take place?

4. What are the people doing?

5. Why are they doing it?

It's important to speak clearly and to think about the grammar and
vocabulary you will use. Before you begin watching, think about these
questions:

1. What tense(s) should you use to describe actions that are happening as
   you are describing them?

2. How will you refer to people? The first time you mention someone you
   might say something like "There is a man in a grey coat." How will you
   refer to him the second time you mention him? What will you say if
   there are several men in grey coats?

Directions to student B:

You are going to be told about a movie. You will not see the movie. Your
partner (student A) will tell you about the movie. Pay close attention. Try to listen
for information to answer the following questions:

1. Who are the people in the scene?

2. Where are the people?

3. When does the scene take place?

4. What are the people doing?

5. Why are they doing it?

Activity 2

Directions to the teacher:

Maintain the pairings from Activity 1. Group all the A students at one end of the room. Group all the B students at the other end of the room. Have the separate groups of A and B students discuss what they saw (or heard) in Activity 1. Then have each student write a paragraph describing the scene. When the students finish talking about and writing their paragraphs, put them in their original pairs. Have them compare and discuss their paragraphs. Check for comprehension in a large group discussion.

Directions to student A:

Write a brief paragraph about what you saw in Activity 1. Remember to include information from these questions:

1. Who were the people in the scene?
2. Where were the people?
3. When did the scene take place?
4. What were the people doing?
5. Why were they doing it?

Directions to student B:

Write a brief paragraph about what you were told in Activity 1. Remember to include information from these questions:

1. Who were the people in the scene?
2. Where were the people?
3. When did the scene take place?
4. What were the people doing?
5. Why were they doing it?

Activity 3

Directions to the teacher:

Keep the students in their pairs. Play the entire scene one time with the sound on. Have the students discuss the question that follows and then check for comprehension in a large group discussion.

Directions to the students:

In your pairs, watch the scene together with the sound on. Discuss the answer to this question:

Why did the man ride across the field?

Scene 2 In the Office

Idiom in this scene

> to be posted

Activity 1

Directions to the teacher:

> *Divide the students into groups of three or four. Play the entire scene one time with the sound off. Have the students discuss the questions and then check for comprehension in a large group discussion.*

Directions to the students:

> With the members of your group, you are going to see a scene from the movie *Dances with Wolves*. The first time you see the scene, the sound will not be on. After you have watched the scene with the other members of your group, discuss the answers to these questions:

> 1. Where are the men?
> 2. What is the relationship between the men?
> 3. What do you think the man who is sitting is doing?
> 4. What do you think the man who is standing thinks about the man who is sitting?
> 5. What do you think the men are talking about?

Activity 2

Directions to the teacher:

> *Maintain the groups from the previous activity. Have the students look up the words, discuss the answer to the question, and write and perform role plays using the words.*

Directions to the students:

> In groups, look up the following words in your dictionary. Discuss them with your teacher and the other students in your group. Then, write and perform a short role play using the words.

> > ascend to a position
> > lad
> > knight
> > realm
> > boon

> What kind of person might use words like this?

Activity 3

Directions to the teacher:

Maintain the groupings from Activity 1. Play the scene one time with the sound on. Have the students discuss the answers to the questions. Check for comprehension in a large group discussion.

Directions to the students:

In your groups, listen to the scene one time with the sound on. Discuss the answers to the questions.

1. What is the relationship between the men?

2. What kind of person is the man who is sitting? What can you tell about him from the words he uses?

3. What do you think the man who is standing thinks about the man who is sitting?

Teaching Point

There are many ways to categorize English questions. They can be divided into standard questions and nonstandard questions.

Standard questions have a verb before the subject. **Nonstandard questions** do not. A nonstandard question is often just a sentence or a word spoken with rising intonation at the end of the sentence.

For example, a standard question might be:

Do you know him?

Nonstandard questions might be:

You know him?
Know him?

Nonstandard questions are often used to request confirmation. This type of question is often a direct restatement of what someone else has already said.

Example: S1 Here's the milk.
S2 Here's the milk? Oh yes. Here's the milk.
(Did I hear you correctly? Did you say "Here's the milk?")

Nonstandard questions are also used to show surprise or disbelief. In this type of question, the voice is louder and one or more words receive a lot of emphasis.

Example: S1 I liked the movie we saw last night.
S2 You liked the movie?
(I'm surprised. I didn't think you liked it.)

Activity 4

Directions to the teacher:

Maintain the groupings from previous activities. Play the entire scene twice with the sound on. Have the students fill in the cloze passage and discuss the questions. Check for comprehension in a large group discussion.

Directions to the students:

Listen to the scene twice. This time, write the questions that you hear. Share your answers with the members of your group.

Seated Man: Lieutenant John J. Dunbar.

_____

Dunbar: Yes, sir.

Seated Man: Yes, sir. _____

Dunbar: Excuse me.

Seated Man: Well it says here that you're to be posted on the frontier. The frontier is Indian country. I quickly deduce that you're an Indian fighter. I did not ascend to this position by being stupid.

Dunbar: No sir.

Seated Man: It says here that you've been decorated.

Dunbar: Yes, sir.

Seated Man: _____

Dunbar: Actually, sir, I'm here at my own request.

Seated Man: _____

Dunbar: I've always wanted to see the frontier.

Seated Man: _____

Dunbar: Yes sir, before it's gone.

Seated Man: Such a smart lad coming straight to me. Sir Knight, I am sending you on a knight's errand. You will report to Captain Hargill at the furthermost outpost of the realm—Fort Sedgewick. My personal seal will assure your safety through many miles of wild and hostile country.

Dunbar: I was wondering…

Seated Man: _____

Dunbar: I was wondering —

Seated Man: _____

Dunbar: No sir.

Seated Man: You think I don't know?

Dunbar: No, sir. It's just that I don't know.

Seated Man: Hold your tongue. I happen to be in a generous mood and I will grant your boon. See that peasant out there? He calls himself Timmons. He's going to your Fort Sedgewick this very afternoon. You can ride with him if you like. He knows the way. Thank you. That is all.

Sir Knight! I have just pissed in my pants and nobody can do anything about it.

Look at the questions that you heard in the scene. Discuss these questions with the members of your group.

Which questions are requesting confirmation of something?

Which express disbelief or surprise?

Which are questions that request information?

Scene 3 With the Wolf

Idioms in this scene:

to never fail to do (something)

bogey man

to made out to be

to not be able to bring (oneself) to (do something)

Activity 1

Directions to the teacher:

Divide the students into As and Bs and send the Bs out of the class or otherwise arrange that they can neither hear nor see the movie. Show the scene once with the sound on to the As.

Directions to student A:

Watch the scene from *Dances with Wolves* carefully. Keep the following questions in mind as you watch the scene. You will need to report what you have seen to a B student.

1. What happens at the beginning, middle, and end of the scene?

2. How are the beginning, middle, and end of the scene connected?

3. Who are the people in the scene?

4. Where does the action take place?

Remember: you will report this scene to your B partner. Before you begin, think about this question:

What tense will you use to tell your B partner about something that you have seen?

Directions to student B:

You will hear a report about the scene. Keep the following questions in mind as you hear the report. If you don't understand something, make sure you ask your A partner to give you the information.

1. What happened at the beginning, middle, and end of the scene?

2. How were the beginning, middle, and end of the scene connected?

3. Who were the people in the scene?

4. Where did the action take place?

Activity 2

Directions to the teacher:

Play the entire scene one time with the sound on for both members of the pairs.

Directions to the students:

With your partner, watch the scene one time with the sound on. Then, discuss the questions again.

1. What happened at the beginning, middle and end of the scene?

2. How were the beginning, middle, and end of the scene connected?

3. Who were the people in the scene?

4. Where did the action take place?

Activity 3

Directions to the teacher:

Maintain the pairings of the previous activities. Play the scene two times. Have the students fill in the parts of the dialogue below. Check for comprehension in a large group discussion.

Directions to the students:

In pairs, listen twice to the dialogue between the white man and the native American. Write the white man's part of the dialogue. Share your notes with your partner. Then, working with your partner, write in English your idea of the native American's part of the dialogue. What do you think he probably said?

Native American: _____?

Dunbar: _____.

_____?

_____?

_____.

_____.

Native American: _____.

Activity 4

Directions to the teacher:

Maintain the pairs. Play the entire scene one more time. Have the students discuss the following questions and then check for comprehension in a large group discussion.

Directions to the students:

In pairs, listen to the dialogue between the native American and the white man. Discuss these questions:

1. Do you think that these two people know each other?

2. How do you know?

Activity 5

Directions to the teacher:

Play the part of the scene in which Dunbar reads his journal entry aloud twice. Put the students in groups of four. Have them discuss the answers to the following questions and then check for comprehension in a large group discussion.

Directions to the students:

In groups of four, listen as Dunbar reads his journal entry. Discuss the answers to the following questions.

1. What has Dunbar been told about the Indians?

2. Who do you think probably told him that?

3. What does Dunbar think about the Indians?

4. How does Dunbar feel about his communication with the Indians?

5. Where is Dunbar going to go?

Scene 4 In the Tent

Activity 1

Directions to the teacher:

Play Scene 4 one time. Put the students in groups of three or four. Have them discuss the answers to the following questions in small groups. Then, check for comprehension in a large group discussion.

Directions to the students:

In groups, listen to the scene one time and discuss the answers to these questions.

1. What does Dunbar want to do?

2. Why does he want to do it?

3. What does Kicking Bird want Dunbar to do?

4. Why do you think Kicking Bird gave Dunbar a new name?

Teaching Point

In translation, the forms of **reported speech** are sometimes used.

**Example: José: Yo quiero comprar una película.
(I want to buy a movie.)**

Translator: He said that he wants to buy a movie.

The verbs *say, tell, want to know,* and *ask* are commonly used in reported speech. Because the translator is standing right next to the person, there is no time change and there is no change in the tense of the speech that is reported.

Activity 2

Directions to the teacher:

Divide the students into pairs of A and B. Have the A students listen to Dunbar's words in English and the B students listen to the woman's words in English. Play the dialogue part of the scene two times. Have students discuss the answers in small groups and then check for comprehension in a large group discussion.

Directions to student A:

You'll hear the scene two times. Listen for Dunbar's words in English. Write them in the spaces provided. Share them with your partner.

Directions to student B:

You'll hear the scene two times. Listen for the woman's words in English. Write them in the spaces provided. Share them with your partner.

Dunbar:
(English)   _____

_____

Kicking Bird: _____

Woman:
(English)   _____

Dunbar:
(English)
Woman: _____

Kicking Bird: _____

Woman:
(English)   _____

Dunbar:
(English)   _____

_____

Woman: _____

Kicking Bird: _____

Woman:
(English)   _____

Dunbar:
(English)   _____

Kicking Bird: _____

Woman: _____
(English)

Dunbar: _____
(English)
Woman: _____

Kicking Bird: _____

Woman: _____
(English)

Dunbar: _____
(English)
Woman: _____
(English)

Dunbar: _____
(English)
Woman: _____

Dunbar: _____

Kicking Bird: _____

Woman: _____

Dunbar: _____

Now, working in pairs, write in English the words that you think Kicking Bird spoke.

Scene 5 At the River

Activity 1

Directions to the teacher:

Put the students into groups of three or four for a global listening. Play the scene one time with the sound on. Have them discuss the lists they generate. Then, check for comprehension in a large group discussion.

Directions to the students:

In groups of three or four, listen to the scene carefully. Then write a list of all the information that you learn about the woman. Try to write at least four things. Share your list with the members of your group and discuss it.

1. _____

2. _____

3. _____

4. _____

Activity 2

Directions to the teacher:

Maintain the groupings from the previous activity. Have the students listen from the point at which Dances with Wolves questions the woman about her name. Play the scene two times. Have the students do the cloze passage and discuss it in small groups. Then, review it in a large group for comprehension.

Directions to the students:

You will hear the scene two times. Write the words that are missing from the following passage. Then, discuss your answers with the members of the group.

Dances with Wolves: _____

Woman: I was not very old when __ came to be with the people _____ I was

made to work. I _____ every day very hard. There was ____ one

... one woman who didn't like _____ much and she used to call

_____ bad names and sometimes she—amapre— _____? me.

Um. One day she was _____ me these bad names with her

_____ in my face and I hit _____. I was not very big but

_____ fell down. She fell hard and _____ move and then I

stood over _____ with my fist and asked if _____ was any other

woman who wanted _____ call me bad names. No one _____

after that day.

Activity 3

Directions to the teacher:

Play the entire scene one time with the sound on. Maintain the groups from the previous activities. Have the students discuss the answers to the following questions. Check for comprehension in a large group discussion.

Directions to the students:

In groups, listen to the scene one time. Then, discuss the answers to these questions:

1. What do you think the woman's name is?
2. How do you think Dunbar got the name Dances with Wolves?

Activity 4

Directions to the teacher:

Maintain the groups from the previous activity. Have the students develop their description of Dunbar/Dances with Wolves and then have them present their descriptions to the entire class.

Directions to the students:

Work in your groups to develop a list of words that describe the personality of Dunbar/Dances with Wolves. Make sure you can explain why you chose those words. Use the information that you have learned about Dunbar in the five scenes that you have seen so far to develop your list. Be prepared to present your list and your reasons to the entire class.

Scene 6 At the Fort

Idiom in this scene

to turn

Activity 1

Directions to the teacher:

Divide the students into three groups: A, B, and C. The As will watch the scene and report it to the Bs, who will report it to the Cs. For the first viewing, with sound, the Bs and Cs should leave the room. Then, call in the B students so that they can hear the first report. Then, call in the C students so they can hear the second report.

Directions to student A:

Watch the scene from Dances with Wolves one time with the following questions in mind:

1. Where does the scene take place?

2. Who are the people in the scene?

3. What do they do in the scene?

4. Why do they do it?

When you have finished watching the scene, you will report it to a B student, who will report it to a C student. What tense will you use to report it?

Directions to student B:

Student A will report to you about the scene. Make sure you understand exactly what you have been told. Keep the following questions in mind:

1. Where did the scene take place?

2. Who were the people in the scene?

3. What did they do in the scene?

4. Why did they do it?

When you have heard partner A's report, you will report it to partner C. What reporting verbs will you use? What tense will you use to make your report?

Directions to student C:

Student B will report to you the scene that student A saw. Make sure you understand exactly what you have been told. Keep the following questions in mind:

1. Where does the scene take place?

2. Who are the people in the scene?

3. What do they do in the scene?

4. Why do they do it?

When you have heard student B's report, you will report it to student A.

Directions to student A:

Compare your report to student B with what you heard from student C. Were there any differences? Explain the differences to students B and C.

Teaching Point

Tag questions are one type of biased English question. Tag questions are a sentence or a part of a sentence followed by a verb and a subject. Tag questions are used by speakers who expect confirmation of what they said.

You are going, aren't you? (I expect you to say "yes.")

Often, when the sounds of the letter *y* follows the sound of the letter *t*, the sound *ch* is produced.

Can't you see the man?
(Sounds like: kanchu see the man?)

Activity 2

Directions to the teacher:

> *Put the students in groups of three or four. Have them fill out the cloze passage and compare answers. Then, check for comprehension in a large group discussion.*

Directions to the students:

In groups, write the questions that you hear in this dialogue. Then, compare your answers with those of the other members of your group.

Sergeant: _____?
Spotty!

Spotty: Yeah, Sergeant?

Sergeant: Tell the major he's waking up. Move your worthless ass.

Voice: Major's coming through.

_____?

Officer 1: _____?

Sergeant: I don't k now sir.

_____?

_____?

TALK!

Dances with Wolves:
I speak English.

Officer 1: _____?

Dances with Wolves:
Lieutenant John J. Dunbar. This is my post.

Officer 1: _____?

Dances with Wolves:
I came out from Fort Hays last April but there was nobody here.

Officer 2: _____?

Dances with Wolves:
My journal's on the bunk in my quarters. My orders are in the journal. It'll…it'll tell you everything.

Officer 2: Spotty, you and Edwards were the first ones here.

_____?

_____?

Spotty: Nah, we didn't find nothing, sir.

Officer 2: _____?

Spotty: He's outside. Hey, he didn't find nothing either.

Office 2:   Somebody find me Edwards.

Sergeant: _____?

Activity 3

Directions to the teacher:

Play the entire scene one more time for the groups. Have them answer the following questions. Then, check for comprehension in a large group discussion.

Directions to the students:

In groups, listen to the scene again. Listen specifically for the tag questions that the Sergeant asks Dunbar. Write the tag questions here. Share your notes and then discuss the questions.

1. _____

What answer does the Sergeant expect?

2. _____

What answer does the Sergeant expect?

Activity 4

Directions to the teacher:

Maintain the groups of students. Play the entire scene one time. Have the students discuss the answers to the following questions. Then check for comprehension in a large group discussion.

Directions to the students:

In groups, listen to the scene one time and discuss the answers to the following questions:

1. What do you think has happened between the previous scene and this scene?

2. How do you know?

Pre-Viewing Questions

Directions:

Consider the following questions as you watch the movie. You will be asked to discuss these questions, as well as others, after you have seen the movie.

1. What is your favorite scene in the movie? Why is it your favorite scene?

2. What is the symbolism of the wolf in the movie?

3. What do you learn about the culture and history of native Americans in this movie?

4. What do you think finally happened to the Sioux?

Post-Viewing Questions

Directions:

Now that you have seen the movie, discuss the answers to the following questions in groups of three or four.

1. Discuss a scene that you did not understand. Ask the members of your group if they can explain it to you.

2. Describe your favorite scene in the movie and explain to the members of your group why it was your favorite scene.

3. Explain the symbolism of the wolf in the movie.

4. Explain to the members of your group something that you have learned about native Americans from watching the movie.

5. Consider the reading "The War for the Black Hills" and the movie. What do you think finally happened to the Sioux?

6. Would you recommend this movie to a friend? Why or why not?

Post-Viewing Activities

1. Find out about the Sioux today. Where do they live? How many are there? What is their life like today? Report on this to your class.

2. Read the complete chapter "The War for the Black Hills" from the book *Bury My Heart at Wounded Knee* by Dee Brown. Report on what you have learned to your class.

3. If you are living in the United States, find out about the nearest nation of native Americans. If they have a reservation, plan a trip to visit the reservation.

4. Read the book *Dances with Wolves* by Michael Blake and report on it to your friends.

If You Liked This Movie

You may want to see these other movies about native Americans in early America:

The Last of the Mohicans (1992) starring Daniel Day Lewis and Russell Means. Directed by Michael Mann (114 min. color)

Black Robe (1992) starring Lothaire Bluteau. Directed by Bruce Beresford (101 min. color).

Chapter 3

United Nations photo

As You Begin

Directions:

Read the following short passage. Look at the picture. Then, in groups of three or four, discuss the questions.

Some countries consist completely of one group of people; however, most countries have several different groups of people. While there may be a predominant group, we can find, in most countries, people who are different than the majority group. We call these groups minority groups. They may look different. They may speak a different language. They may have different customs. These groups often lend a certain spice to a country that would be somewhat bland without them.

1. Name some countries which have minority groups and give the names of those groups.

2. In what ways are the minority groups different than the majority group?

3. Are people from these minority groups treated differently than other people? Are they discriminated against? Are they offered any special protections?

A Reading to Get Things Started

Directions:

Read the following passage. Use your dictionary to find words that you don't know. After you have finished reading, discuss the answers to the questions with a classmate or a small group of your classmates.

I Have a Dream

In 1963, Dr. Martin Luther King, Jr., the foremost American civil rights leader, gave what was to become his most famous speech in Washington, D.C. This is an excerpt from that speech:

I say to you today, my friends, so even though we face the difficulties of today and tomorrow, I still have a dream. It is a dream deeply rooted in the American dream.

I have a dream that one day this nation will rise up and live out the true meaning of its creed: "We hold these truths to be self-evident: that all men are created equal."

I have a dream that one day on the red hills of Georgia the sons of former slaves and the sons of former slaveowners will be able to sit down together at the table of brotherhood; I have a dream —

That one day even the state of Mississippi, a state sweltering with the heat of injustice, sweltering with the heat of oppression, will be transformed into an oasis of freedom and justice; I have a dream—

That my four little children will one day live in a nation where they will not be judged by the color of their skin but by the content of their character; I have a dream today.

I have a dream that one day down in Alabama, with its vicious racists, with its governor having his lips dripping with the words of interposition and nullification, one day right there in Alabama little black boys and black girls will be able to join hands with little white boys and white girls as sisters and brothers; I have a dream today.

I have a dream that one day every valley shall be exalted, every hill and mountain shall be made low, and rough places will be made plane and crooked places will be made straight, and the glory of the Lord shall be revealed, and all flesh shall see it together.

This is our hope. This is the faith that I go back to the South with. With this faith we will be able to hew out of the mountain of despair a stone of hope. With this faith we will be able to transform the jangling discords of our nation into a beautiful symphony of brotherhood. With this faith we will be able to work together, to pray together, to struggle together, to go to jail together, to stand up for freedom together, knowing that we will be free one day.

This will be the day… This will be the day when all of God's children will be able to sing with new meaning. "My country 'tis of thee, sweet land of liberty, of thee I sing. Land where my fathers died, land of the pilgrim's pride, from every mountainside, let freedom ring," and if America is to be a great nation—this must become true.

So let freedom ring—from the prodigious hilltops of New Hampshire, let freedom ring; from the mighty mountains of New York, let freedom ring; from the heightening Alleghenies of Pennsylvania!

Let freedom ring from the snowcapped Rockies of Colorado!

Let freedom ring from the curvaceous slopes of California!

But not only that; let freedom ring from Stone Mountain of Georgia!

Let freedom ring from Lookout Mountain of Tennessee!

Let freedom ring from every hill and molehill of Mississippi. From every mountainside, let freedom ring, and when this happens…

When we allow freedom to ring, when we let it ring from every village and hamlet, from every state and every city, we will be able to speed up that day when all of God's children, black men and white men, Jews and Gentiles, Protestants and Catholics, will be able to join hands and sing in the words of the old Negro spiritual, "Free at last, free at last; thank God almighty, we are free at last."

Questions for Discussion

1. Where do you think the words, "We hold these truths to be self-evident: that all men are created equal" might come from?

2. Dr. King gives many illustrations of his dream. Which do you find the most powerful? Why?

3. When Dr. King says that he wants freedom to ring for "black men and white men, Jews and Gentiles, Protestants and Catholics," what does he mean?

4. What does "let freedom ring" mean?

5. Dr. King gave this speech in 1963. What progress towards his dream do you think has been made in the United States since then?

Idioms from the Film, *To Kill a Mockingbird*

Activity 1

Directions to the teacher:

Read the following list of idioms and have students repeat them for correct pronunciation.

Directions to the students:

Listen as your teacher reads the list of idioms below. Pay attention to the teacher's pronunciation. Then study the list. These idioms are from the video scenes you will be working with.

1. judging from ↔ considering

Definition: considering, taking into account

Example: *Judging from* the weather forecast, it should be a nice day.

Example from the film: Well *judging from* his tracks he's about six and a half feet tall.

2. to defend ↔ to be the defense lawyer for someone who is accused of a crime

Definition: to act as the defense lawyer for someone accused of a crime

Example: He *defended* a man accused of stealing a car.

Example from the film: Cap'n I'm real sorry that they picked you *to defend* that nigger that raped my Mayella.

3. to save (someone) a lot of trouble ↔ to help (someone) avoid a problem

Definition: to help someone avoid a problem

Example: My new computer *saved me a lot of trouble* when I was writing this book.

Example from the film: I would have *saved you* and the sheriff and the taxpayers *lots of trouble.*

4. dead ↔ completely

Definition: completely, absolutely, totally

Example: He was *dead* right in his prediction.

Example from the film: I said you wrong man. You *dead* wrong.

5. ain't ◆→ isn't, aren't

Definition: am not, is not, are not

Example: I *ain't* going to listen to him any more.

Example from the film: Mr. Finch *ain't* taking his story against our'n.

Language note: This idiom is used in very informal speech and is sometimes considered non-standard or uneducated English

---

6. charged ◆→ accused

Definition: to be officially accused of a crime

Example: He is *charged* with murder.

Example from the film: I've been appointed to defend Tom Robinson. Now that he's been *charged* that's what I intend to do.

7. to (sing) (one's) hearts out ◆→ to (do) (their) best

Definition: to do one's utmost, particularly to please others

Example: The team *played their hearts out* for the coach.

Example from the film: They don't do one thing but just *sing their hearts out* for us.

8. to come over ◆→ to go to visit someone

Definition: to come or go to visit someone at their place

Example: Can you *come over* to my house for dinner?

Example from the film: I *came over* to tell you about my visit with Tom.

9. to cool down ◆→ to become more calm or rational

Definition: to become calm after having been angry

Example: I wish everyone would just stop shouting and *cool down* a little.

Example from the film: And to let you know I got a postponement of the trial to give things a chance to *cool down*.

10. all bluff ◆→ nothing substantial

Definition: used to describe someone who makes a lot of noise, but who is unlikely to actually do anything

Example: His threats are *all bluff*.

Example from the film: He's *all bluff*.

Activity 2

Directions to the teacher:

Have students read the following sentences. Instruct them to rewrite the sentences, replacing the items in bold print with one of the idioms from the list in Activity 1.

Directions to the students:

Read the sentences that follow. Then rewrite the sentences replacing the items in bold text with idioms from Activity 1.

1. **Considering** the seriousness of the crime he has been **accused of**, I would think that he would want the best possible attorney to **represent** him.

   _____

   _____

   _____

2. I **am here** to tell you that, although your business partner is very upset, he is willing to talk with you. I think he has **calmed down** a lot since yesterday. I think you both could have **avoided a lot of trouble for yourselves** if you hadn't started shouting at each other. I know he thinks that you're wrong. And I know you think he's **completely** wrong. But you have to sit down and talk about this.

   _____

   _____

   _____

Activity 3

Directions to the teacher:

Have the students work in pairs to complete the following dialogues using at least one idiom from Activity 1. After you have checked their work, have them practice the dialogues with their partners.

Directions to the students:

Work with a partner to complete the following dialogues. Be sure to use at least one idiom from Activity 1 in each dialogue. After your teacher has checked your work, practice your dialogue with your partner.

1. Situation: Amy and Rick are talking about Rick's landlord.

   Rick: I don't know what it's all about. Early this morning, the police came and took him away. They put handcuffs on him and took him away. I don't know what's going on.

   Amy: _____

   _____

2. Situation: Nancy and Mary are talking about the Bake Sale that they were involved with.

   Nancy: It was such a success. Why, we raised over $200. Everybody did such a great job.

   Mary: _____

   _____

3. Situation: Vic arrived at his office this morning to find a police officer there. His computer was missing and all of the drawers in his desk had been emptied. The window behind his desk was broken and there were drops of dried blood on the floor.

Vic: What happened officer?

Officer: _____

             _____

4. Situation: Bill is talking with Martha about his neighbor.

Bill: He just doesn't like my dog. Yesterday he told me that he's going to call the police the next time he hears her bark. He's even threatened to sue me over the noise. I just don't know what to do.

Martha: _____

             _____

5. Situation: Dave is at home alone. It's 10 o'clock in the evening. The doorbell rings. Dave is surprised. He's not expecting any visitors. He opens the door, and finds his cousin Allen standing at the door.

Dave: Allen, what is it? Is something wrong?

Allen: _____

             _____

Scene 1 Jem & Dill Talk about Boo

Idiom in this scene:

judging from

Photofest

Teaching Point

Certain words in an English sentence will seem to JUMP out of the sentence. These words are usually the longer words in the sentence—the nouns, adjectives, adverbs, and verbs. These words are called **content words**, and, in most English sentences, they are the easiest words to hear.

Activity 1

Directions to the teacher:

Place the students in pairs or small groups. Have them watch the scene once with the sound on. Check for comprehension in a large group discussion.

Directions to the students:

In pairs or small groups, watch the scene one time. Write down some of the words the children use to describe what they are talking about. Share your notes with the members of your groups.

_____

_____

Discuss the answer to the following question:

Are the children talking about a person or a thing? How do you know?

Activity 2

Directions to the teacher:

Cue the scene to the part where the son begins the description of Boo. Pair the students or put them in small groups. Check for comprehension in a large group discussion.

Directions to the students:

As you watch the scene, fill in the missing words of the dialogue. Share your answers with the other students in your group. Then, discuss the answer to the question that follows.

Jem: Well judging from his tracks he's about _____ _____. He eats _____ and all the _____ he can catch. There's a _____ jagged _____that runs all the way across his face. His teeth are _____ and _____. His _____ are _____, and he _____most of the time.

Discussion Question

What was Dill's (the listener's) reaction to the description of Boo?

Activity 3

Directions to the teacher:

Pair or group the students. Have them watch the entire scene one time. Check for comprehension in a large group discussion.

Directions to the student:

Work in pairs or small groups. Discuss the answers to these questions after you watch the scene.

1. According to Jem, is Boo dangerous?
2. Do you think Boo is dangerous?
3. There is another person in this scene. Who is it? What relationship do you think this person has with the two boys?

Scene 2   Atticus & Ewell outside the Courtroom

to defend
to save (someone) trouble
dead
ain't
to be charged

Activity 1

Directions to the teacher:

Pair the students. Show the entire scene one time with the sound off. Have each pair produce an "action script" of the activity in the scene. Then, have one member of each pair narrate the action script to the entire class.

Directions to the students:

In pairs, watch the entire scene one time. Then, write an action script of the activity in the scene. As you prepare your script, discuss and try to answer these questions:

1. What happens first? second? third?
2. Who are the people in the scene?
3. What is the man in the hat trying to do?
4. What is the man in the suit trying to do?
5. How does this scene "feel"? Is it happy? Sad? Tense?
6. What is the attitude of the man in the hat at the end of the scene?
7. How can you describe the face of the man in the suit from the beginning to the end of the scene?

Activity 2

Directions to the teacher:

Put students in pairs or small groups. Have the students look up the following words in their dictionaries. Have the students discuss the questions that follow the first word. For words 2 to 4, the students in each group should prepare a small role play which they can perform in front of the entire class.

Directions to the students:

In pairs or small groups look up the following words in an English-English dictionary. For word 1, discuss the answers to the questions. For words 2 to 4 write and perform short role-plays in front of your class using those words.

1. nigger

   Is this a polite word? How do you know?
   To what group of people does this word refer?
   What does it tell you about the type of person who uses it?
   What is the correct term to refer to people of this group?

2. rape

3. save (someone) trouble

4. intend to do something

Activity 3

Directions to the teacher:

Put students in pairs. Show the entire scene one time with the sound on. Have the students work in pairs to fill in the following cloze passage. Check for comprehension in a large group discussion.

Directions to the students:

In pairs, watch the scene one time with the sound on. Work with your partner to fill in the missing words of the dialogue.

Mr. Ewell: Cap'n, I'm real _____ that they _____ you to defend that _____ that _____ my Mayella. I don't know why I didn't kill him myself instead of going to the sheriff. I would have saved you and the sheriff and the taxpayers lots of trouble.

Mr. Finch: _____

Mr. Ewell: Hey, Cap'n. Somebody told me just now that they _____ that you _____ Tom Robinson's story against our'n. You know what I said? I said, "you _____ man. You _____wrong. Mr. Finch ain't taking his story against our'n. Well they _____ wrong, _____ they?

Mr. Finch: I've been _____ to defend Tom Robinson. Now that he's been _____ that's what I _____ to do.

Mr. Ewell: You _____ his story?

Mr. Finch: If you'll excuse me Mr. Ewell?

Mr. Ewell: What _____ of man _____ you? You got children of your own.

Teaching point:

Sometimes in informal speech we "quote" ourselves to make a point more emphatically. **Self-quotation** is often done after asking a rhetorical question. For example, if you are trying to emphasize that you refused to do something very strongly, you might say:

He asked me to lie, and you know what I said? I said, "There's no way I'm going to lie for you."

Activity 4

Directions to the teacher:

Have students work individually to write a short monologue using self-quotation for emphasis. Then have them check each others' sentences and practice them in pairs.

Directions to the students:

Based on the situation described below, write a short monologue in which you use self-quotation for emphasis.

Someone asked you to let them see your paper during a test and you refused.

_____

_____

Now have a partner check your work and then practice your monologue with a partner.

Teaching Point

Implication is a way of saying something indirectly. There are many ways to imply: by using stress, by choice of words, and by intonation.

Examples:

by using stress: You *liked* that book.
                          (implies that the speaker didn't like the book and/or can't believe you did like the book)

by choice of words: He *calls* himself a lawyer.
                          (implies that the speaker doesn't think he's a good lawyer)

by intonation: You're going to marry *Fred?*
                          (implies that the speaker is surprised by your choice)

Activity 5

Directions to the teacher:

Place the students in pairs or small groups. Have them discuss the answers to the following questions. Check for comprehension in a large group discussion.

Directions to the students:

In pairs or small groups, discuss the answers to the following questions:

1. What does Mr. Ewell imply when he says "I would have saved you and the sheriff and the taxpayers lots of trouble?" How does Mr. Ewell make this implication—by stress, by choice of words, or by intonation?

2. What does Mr. Ewell imply when he says "What kind of man are you? You got children of your own"? How does Mr. Ewell make this implication—by stress, by choice of words, or by intonation?

Activity 6

Directions to the teacher:

Place the students in pairs or small groups. Play the scene two more times. Have them fill out the following chart and discuss their answers. Check for comprehension in a large group discussion.

Directions to the students:

You will hear the scene two more times. In pairs or small groups, fill out the following chart. Discuss your answers with your partner.

Mr. Ewell's attitude towards Mr. Finch changes as this scene progresses. His attitude can be divided into three parts.

Part	Attitude	Words which signalled it
Beginning	_____	_____
Middle	_____	_____
End	_____	_____

Activity 7

Directions to the teacher:

Put students in pairs or small groups, and have them draw lines between the characters they have been introduced to so far. On the lines they should write the type of relationship (e.g., mother/son, doctor/patient).

Directions to the students:

Draw lines between the characters who have relationships with each other. On the lines write the type of relationship. One has been done for you as an example.

Atticus Finch

Mr. Ewell

Tom Robinson

Jem ——— *brother / sister* ——— Scout

Mayella

Dill

Boo Radley

Scene 3 The Children near the Radley House

Activity 1

Directions to the teacher:

> *Show the first part of the scene (from when the kids are crouching behind the fence until they run away) with the sound off. Divide students into pairs and position them so that only one of the pair, the A student, can see the scene. When the students have finished working in pairs, show the same part of the scene with the sound on, letting both A and B students see the screen. Note that students are asked to describe the action as if it were already finished. You may find it useful to review the appropriate past tenses before proceeding with this exercise.*

Directions to student A:

Watch the segment of the video and describe what you are seeing to your partner as you see it. Describe the action as if it were already finished when you describe it.

Directions to student B:

Listen to your partner's description of the scene, which you will not be able to see. Take notes about what your partner tells you.

Directions to students A and B:

When you finish talking, each of you should write a paragraph about the scene. Write the paragraphs without consulting each other. When you have finished, read each other's paragraphs and discuss any differences or omissions.

Now watch the scene again with the sound on.

Activity 2

Directions to the teacher:

> *Show the second part of the scene (from when they run away until the boy goes back and finds his pants) with the sound off. Have the students in the same pairs change position so that those who were As become Bs and visa versa. When the students have finished working in pairs, show the same part of the scene with the sound, on letting both students see the screen.*

Directions to student A:

Watch the segment of the video and describe what you are seeing to your partner as you see it. Describe the action as if it were already finished when you describe it.

Directions to student B:

Listen to your partner's description of the scene, which you will not be able to see. Take notes about what your partner tells you.

Directions to students A and B:

When you finish talking, each of you should write a paragraph about the scene. Write the paragraphs without consulting each other. When you have finished, read each other's paragraphs and discuss any differences or omissions.

Now watch the scene again with the sound on.

Activity 3

Directions to the teacher:

Have students work individually to prepare to tell a real story from their past. Have them work with partners to clarify their stories.

Directions to the students:

Take a few minutes and write some notes to yourself about a story from your past. In preparing to tell the story, you may wish to answer the following questions. Remember: you will probably want to tell your story in the past tense.

1. When did it take place? (How old were you?)
2. Where did it take place?
3. Besides you, who else was involved in the story?
4. What happened?
5. What did you learn from this experience?

Activity 4

Directions to the teacher:

Put students in pairs and have them tell each other their stories from Activity 3. Encourage students to ask questions for clarification if they don't understand their partners.

Directions to student A:

Tell your story to your partner. Pause after each sentence to allow for questions.

Directions to student B:

Listen to your partner's story and ask questions to be sure you understand. Some questions you may wish to ask are listed next.

What do you mean?

What do you mean by ———?

I'm sorry, I didn't follow you. Could you explain that again?

Directions to students A and B:

Now change roles. The B students will tell their stories and the A students will listen.

Scene 4 The Dining Room at the Finch Home

Idiom from this scene:

(sing) (their) hearts out

Activity 1

Directions to the teacher:

Put students in pairs. Show the entire scene one time with the sound on. Have the students discuss the questions at the end of the scene. Check for comprehension in a large group discussion.

Directions to the students:

In pairs, listen to the scene one time. Keep these questions in mind as you listen to the scene. Then, discuss the questions at the end of the scene.

1. Who are these people?
2. What are their relationships to each other?
3. What are some of the subjects they are discussing?

Teaching Point

The words *say* and *tell* are called **reported speech markers** because they are used to talk about discussions.

Activity 2

Directions to the teacher:

Cue to the clip of dialog in which Atticus is talking in response to Jem's first question. Put the students in pairs. Have them listen one time and discuss the question that follows. Check for comprehension in a large group discussion.

Directions to the students:

In pairs, listen to the piece of dialogue. Listen for the reported speech markers. Discuss the answer to this question:

Who is the man talking about?

Teaching Point

After reporting verbs such as *say* and *tell* you will often hear **verb pattern markers** such as *that* and *to*. For example, all of the following patterns are possible after *say*.

She said that she liked him.
She said to go.

After *tell* many patterns are possible:

She told him the truth.
She told the truth.
She told him that the truth was important.

Activity 3

Directions to the teacher:

Pair the students and play Atticus' first answer three times. Have the students fill in the missing information. Check for comprehension in a large group discussion.

Directions to the students:

In pairs, listen to the clip of dialogue three times. Work with your partner to fill in the missing information.

The person told Atticus

    1. that _____

    2. and that _____

The person said

    1. that _____

    2. that _____

    3. to _____

Teaching Point

In English, there are two types of words: content words and function words. Content words are nouns, main verbs, adjectives, and adverbs. Function words are the small words in a sentence: helping verbs, articles, prepositions, pronouns.

English usually puts the most stress on the last content word of the sentence. The content words in this sentence have (*) over them. The last content word, trees, has a • over it to show that it gets extra emphasis.

       *   *   *   *   •

Mockingbirds usually live in old trees.

However, there are some occasions when there is a difference in the pattern. For example, when we have lists, the items in the list will get equal emphasis. They will seem to JUMP out of the sentence. There will be a pause between each item in the list and the word *and* before the last item in the list. Listen as your teacher reads this sentence:

      *   *   *   •   •   •

Mockingbirds usually live in trees, barns, and attics.

If each of these list items is expanded to make a phrase, the content words in each phrase will receive equal emphasis and there will be a pause after each list item.

Listen as your teacher reads the following sentence:

      *   *   *   *   *   •

Mockingbirds usually live in trees in large forests

          *   *   •

barns in rural areas

         *   *   •

and attics in urban areas.

Activity 4

Directions to the teacher:

> *Cue to the clip of Atticus' second response to Jem. Pair the students. Play the clip two times. Have them fill in the answers. Check for comprehension in a large group discussion.*

Directions to the students:

In pairs, listen to the clip two times. In the clip, the man, Atticus, lists some activities of mockingbirds. With your partner, listen for the list of activities. Fill in the chart. Discuss your answers.

According to Atticus, mockingbirds:

1. _____

2. _____

3. _____

4. _____

Teaching Point

Speech fillers are words that are not really important to the meaning or the grammar of the sentence. For example, in the following dialogue, the words of course are a speech filler.

A: You could listen to the scene again.

B: *Of course*, if that's too hard you can always look at the script in the back of the book.

C: Thanks for the suggestions.

Activity 5

Directions to the teacher:

> *Cue to Atticus' second answer. Pair the students and have them fill in the answers. Check for comprehension in a large group discussion.*

Directions to the students:

In pairs, listen to the first three words. With your partner, fill in the words and discuss the answers to the questions.

Atticus: Well __ _____ _____
                   1   2   3

1. Can you think of other speech fillers that could be used instead of word 2? List them here:

   _____

   _____

   _____

2. Word 3 is a reduction of another word. What word is word 3 reduced from?

   _____

Activity 6

Directions to the teacher:

Cue to the beginning of the scene. Put the students in pairs. Have them listen to the entire scene again and discuss the answer to the question. Then, discuss the answer in a large group.

Directions to the students:

In pairs, listen to the entire scene again. With your partner, discuss the answer to the following question:

Why, according to Atticus, is it a sin to kill a mockingbird?

Scene 5 The Mad Dog

Activity 1

Directions to the teacher:

Put students in pairs or small groups, and have them answer the following questions. Review the answers in a large group. As a follow-up, you may wish to test vocabulary by giving each student a word and having him/her demonstrate the motion to the others to see if they can guess the words.

Directions to the students:

In pairs or small groups, develop a list of five different words that are similar in meaning to the verbs *walk*, *run*, and *go*. Make notes to show how each verb is different in meaning. An example is done for you.

Verbs that mean *walk*

	word	meaning
1.	Saunter	Walk slowly, walk in an unhurried way
2.	_____	_____
3.	_____	_____
4.	_____	_____
5.	_____	_____

Verbs that mean *run*

	word	meaning
1.	_____	_____
2.	_____	_____
3.	_____	_____
4.	_____	_____
5.	_____	_____

Verbs that mean *go*

	word	meaning
1.	_____	_____
2.	_____	_____
3.	_____	_____
4.	_____	_____
5.	_____	_____

Activity 2

Directions to the teacher:

   Put the students in pairs or small groups. Have them look up the special vocabulary and answer the questions. Check for comprehension in a large group discussion.

Directions to the students:

   In pairs or small groups, look up the special vocabulary and discuss the answers to the questions.

1.   Rabies.   What is the part of speech?   _____

              What is the definition?   _____

              What is the adjective form of the word?   _____

              Do you have a problem with rabies in your
              country? If so, how does your government
              control the problem   _____

2.   Aim.   What are the parts of speech?   _____

              What is the definition of the verb form?   _____

              Say a sentence in which you use the verb form.

Teaching Point

   In Chapter 1, Scene 1, Activity 1, you worked with **confirmation questions**. There are many different ways to use confirmation questions. Confirmation questions are questions that you can use when you are not sure you understood something you heard. Here are some common confirmation questions:

   Either/or questions

      Did the boy *run* or *walk*? (If you use this, make sure your voice goes up on the word *run*, and down on the word *walk*. Also, pause before the word *or*)

      Did the boy run or walk?

   Requests for restatement

      Could you tell me again the part about the man?

      I'm not too clear about what happened to the man. Could you repeat that part?

Activity 3

Directions to the teacher:

> *Divide the students into pairs of A and B. Follow these directions for a silent narration: Have student A face the video screen. Have student B sit next to student A, but facing away from the video screen. Play the entire clip with the sound off.*

Directions to student A:

You will explain the scene to your partner, who will not see it. Consider which tense you will use. Try to use at least three of the words you learned in Activity 1.

Directions to student B:

After you have heard about the scene from your viewing partner, ask confirmation questions to make sure you understood what he or she said.

Activity 4

Directions to the teacher:

> *Put all the viewing partners from the previous activity in one group and all the listening partners in another. Have each group write a group report of the scene. Each group should be instructed to elect a spokesperson to read the group report to the entire class. When the report of the viewing partners is read, the listening partners can ask questions and/or make changes. When the report of the listening partners is read, the viewing partners can ask questions and/or make changes.*

Directions to the students:

After your teacher assigns groups, discuss the scene. Write up a group report of the scene. Elect a spokesperson from your group to read the report to the entire class.

Activity 5

Directions to the teacher:

> *Put the students back in their original pairs from Activity 3. Play the entire scene one time with the sound off so that both members of each pair can see it. Have the students discuss it after they have viewed it.*

Directions to the students:

With your partner from Activity 3, watch the entire scene. Discuss the scene with your partner.

Scene 6 Atticus & Jem at the Robinsons'

Idioms in this scene:

to come over

to cool down

all bluff

Teaching Points

There are many ways to **divide a description**. One common way to do it is to use cardinal numbers, such as

In the first part _____
In the second part _____

Adjective clauses are a good way to distinguish between people. For example, in scene 2, you could say

The white man who is wearing a suit…
The white man who is poorly dressed…

to distinguish between the two white men in the scene.

Another way to check your own comprehension is to briefly restate what you thought you heard the other person say and then ask for confirmation about whether you understood correctly.

For example, if a speaker says

In scene 4, there is a father and a group of kids sitting at a table and talking about why it is wrong to kill mockingbirds

you could say:

So a family is discussing why it is wrong to kill a mockingbird. Did I get that right?

Other confirmation questions include

Is that what you said?
Is that correct?

Activity 1

Directions to the teacher:

Group the students in triads. Have two students in each triad leave the room. The third student should watch the entire scene once with the sound turned off. This member will report the entire scene to the other two members when they return at the end of the scene. The two members who did not view the scene will then write up a short report of the scene as it was told to them by the member who did watch it.

Directions to the student who will watch the scene:

In retelling the scene to the other two members of your group, you may wish to divide the scene into parts. Be careful to distinguish between the people in the scene.

Directions to the students who will be told about the scene:

Make sure you understand what the viewing member tells you. Use the confirmation strategies you have learned to verify what you are told. After you have spoken to the viewing member of your group, work together to write up a brief report of what you heard and give it to your teacher.

Teaching Point

A speaker can use many different ways to indicate reasons. One way is to use the **infinitive** form of the verb. For example, a speaker could say either of the following sentences to show his or her reasons for quitting smoking:

I quit smoking because it's bad for my health.

I quit smoking *to protect* my health.

Infinitives are structures made up of both function and content words. It is usually easy to hear the content word (the simple verb) because it is stressed and somewhat harder to hear the function word (the word *to*) because it is not stressed. Because it is not stressed, the vowel sound in to is often reduced to a sound somewhat like "uh" ("tuh"). Listen as your teacher reads these sentences. Can you hear the function word?

I came *to talk* to you.

I need *to go* now.

Activity 2

Directions to the teacher:

Group the students in triads. Cue the scene to the beginning and play it with the sound on until Atticus has gone inside Helen's house. Have the students answer the questions and check for comprehension in a large group discussion.

Directions to the students:

In groups of three listen to the clip your teacher plays for you. Listen for infinitives. Share your answers.

What were Atticus's reasons for visiting Helen?

1. _____

2. _____

Activity 3

Directions to the teacher:

> *Cue the tape to the point at which Atticus has gone inside Helen's house. Play it until the point at which Atticus comes outside. Keep the students in groups of three. Have the students develop the answer to the question. Check for comprehension in a large group discussion.*

Directions to the students:

In groups of three, listen to the clip. Answer the question. Share your answers with your group members.

Jem, the white boy, makes a request. Write the words he uses to make his request.

_____

What are three other ways he could have made the same request?

1. _____

2. _____

3. _____

Activity 4

Directions to the teacher:

> *Cue to the point at which Atticus is carrying Scout onto the front porch. Play it with the sound on until the end of the scene. Keep the students in their groups of three. Have them answer the questions and discuss their answers. Check for comprehension in a large group discussion.*

Directions to the students:

In groups of three, watch the scene and answer the following questions. Share your answers with your group members.

1. Atticus makes two requests, one of the maid and one of his son. Write the words he uses to make his request of the maid.

_____

Can you give another way that he could have made the same request?

_____

2. Write the words he uses to make his request of his son.

_____

Can you give another way that he could have made the same request?

_____

Of the two requests he made, which is more like a command? Why?

_____

Activity 5

Directions to the teacher:

> *Play the entire scene to the entire class with the sound on. Have the students discuss the answers to the questions in groups of three. Check for comprehension in a large group discussion.*

Directions to the students:

> With the members of your group, watch the entire scene one time and discuss the answers to these questions:
>
> Who do you think put the items in the tree? Why?
>
> What do you think will happen next?

Pre-Viewing Questions

1. A major theme of this film is how people should act under difficult circumstances. As you watch the film, keep track of the difficulties that the characters face. What are the "problematic situations" and how do the characters deal with them?

2. Another theme in this film is the issue of raising a child to be a responsible member of society. As you watch the film, try to identify things that Atticus does to raise his children "correctly."

3. The issue of race and racial discrimination is the central moral dilemma in *To Kill a Mockingbird*. In the film, there seem to be certain expectations, among both blacks and whites, about justice for black people. As you watch the film, try to identify what those assumptions are.

4. The issue of "killing a mockingbird" comes up at two points in the film. Pay special attention to these scenes.

5. All societies have things that are openly acknowledged and other things which are kept hidden. In the town in this film, there are many "secrets." As you watch the film, try to identify what these secrets are.

Post-Viewing Questions

1. What "problematic situations" did the following characters face, and how did they deal with them?

Character	Situation	How the character dealt with it
Atticus	_____	_____
	_____	_____
		_____
		_____
Jem	_____	_____
	_____	_____
		_____
		_____
Mr. Ewell	_____	_____
	_____	_____
		_____
		_____
Mayella	_____	_____
	_____	_____
		_____
		_____

2. Through his words and actions, Atticus tries to teach Jem and Scout the correct way to behave. List some of the principles Atticus tries to teach them and the way he teaches them. When you finish, discuss these ideas in small groups. Are these the same things you would wish to teach your own children? Would you teach them in the same way?

What he tried teach them   **How he taught them**

_____   _____

                                            _____

_____   _____

                                            _____

_____   _____

                                            _____

_____   _____

                                            _____

3. What are the expectations that the people had about black people and their rights? Do you think this is still true? If so, why? If not, how have people's expectations changed?

4. Why was this film entitled _To Kill a Mockingbird_?

5. What secrets do the following characters have?

Atticus   _____

Jem   _____

Mr. Ewell   _____

Mayella   _____

The Radley family _____

Post-Viewing Activities

1. Go to the library and look up Martin Luther King, Jr.'s "I Have a Dream" speech. Read it in its entirety. If possible, watch a video of the speech.
2. Go to the library and look up the case of the Scottsboro boys. Report back to the class on what you found out.
3. This film is based on the novel _To Kill a Mockingbird_ by Harper Lee. Divide the book into sections and have each person in the class read one section. Each person could then tell the story of his or her section to the class in sequence.

If You Liked This Film

You may wish to see these other films about racial issues in the American South:

In the Heat of the Night (1967) starring Sidney Poitier and Rod Steiger. Directed by Norman Jewison (109 min. color).

Roots (miniseries) (1977) starring LeVar Burton (color).

Mississippi Burning (1988) starring Gene Hackman and Willem Dafoe. Directed by Alan Parker (125 min. color).

Chapter 4

Library of Congress

As You Begin

Directions:

Read the following short passage. Look at the picture. Then, in groups of three or four, discuss the questions.

A refugee is, by definition, a person without a country. While most of us enjoy the safety and security that a passport and the right to live in one's own country represent, there are large numbers of refugees from various countries who have no place to call home. The United Nations High Commission on Refugees and other organizations try to help these refugees, but they are faced with the basic dilemma that the real solution, which is return to their own countries, is often impossible.

1. Name countries from which refugees are coming today.

2. Name some countries from which refugees have come in the past.

3. What conditions create a refugee population?

4. What solutions do refugees seek for their problem?

5. Does your country accept refugees? If so, from what countries and under what conditions?

A Reading to Get Things Started

Directions:

Read the following passage. Use your dictionary to find words that you don't know. After you have finished reading, discuss the answers to the questions with a classmate or a small group of your classmates. Check the vocabulary list before you begin.

Vocabulary List

Gestapo - The German secret police during World War II.

Vichy France

During much of World War II, France was divided into two parts: Occupied France (mostly in the north and headquartered in Paris) and Vichy France (mostly in the south and headquartered in the resort city of Vichy). Vichy France was a *puppet* government. Nominally, it was controlled by the French, but in reality, it was controlled by the French who strongly supported the Germans. Because Vichy France was nominally in control of the French, countries that were at war with the Germans were able to maintain diplomatic missions there. The Americans, for instance, kept a legation in Vichy France as late as 1942, long after America had entered the war again Germany, which occupied the northern part of France.

Vichy France provided an escape route for many people fleeing from German occupied Europe. The following excerpt, taken from the book *War and Remembrance*, details the dilemma of the American consul, Jim Gaither, at Marseille:

Pouring more whiskey and soda, Gaither thought of a leading article in *Le Cahier Jaune*, the French anti-Semitic journal that he had glanced through on the train coming back from Vichy. The photographs had been taken at a French government exhibit in Paris called "Jewish Traits and Physiognomies": huge plaster models of hook noses, blubber lips, and protruding ears. Louis Henry didn't fit the specifications; but if French immigration inspectors, or the **Gestapo**, laid hands on him, he would be a Jew like his mother. Otherwise of course, Mrs. Henry could bluff her way through any border point, even without the lieutenant; a beautiful woman, a mother, an American; ordinarily no problem! But the Germans had turned routine travel in Europe, for Jews, into a risk like jumping from a burning building. Trivial bits of paper could mean life or death; Gaither knew Jews with valid passports and exit visas who were staying on in France merely for fear of facing the Gestapo at the borders.

The silence in the rooms was leaden as Gaither passed the drinks. To ease the strain, he talked about how he had gotten British pilots out of France on this train to Barcelona, posing as firemen and engineers. But they were tough men, he explained, trained in the escape art, prepared to confront the Gestapo; and still there had been some bad incidents...

From *War and Remembrance* by Herman Wouk. Copyright © 1978 by Herman Wouk. By permission of Little, Brown and Co.

Questions for Discussion

1. What is the problem that Gaither is worried about?

2. Who is Mrs. Henry? What do you know about her?

3. What kinds of people has Gaither helped to escape? How had he helped them?

4. How do the Germans and the Vichy French identify Jews?

5. What papers did Jews need to leave Vichy France?

Idioms from the Film, *Casablanca*

Directions to the teacher:

   Read the following list of idioms and have students repeat them for correct pronunciation.

Activity 1

Directions to the students:

Listen as your teacher reads the following list of idioms. Pay attention to the teacher's pronunciation. Then study the list. These idioms are from the video scenes you will be working with.

1. to *round up* ◆◆ to collect people, especially criminals

Definition: To collect people into a group. The word is often used by police to refer to arresting a group of criminals.

Ex. Mother to child: *Round up* your brothers and sisters and we'll go see a movie.

Ex. from the film: *Round up* all suspicious characters and search them for stolen documents.

2. a *lucky break* ◆◆ an incidence of good fortune or luck

Definition: an opportunity in which a person experiences luck or good fortune

Ex. Student to student: It was *a lucky break* for me that the test question was exactly what I had studied for.

Ex. from the film: They got a *lucky break*.

3. to *beat* someone's *price* ◆◆ to offer at a lower price

Definition: to offer something at a lower price than one's competitors

Ex. Sign on a grocery store: We *beat* our competitors' *prices*. We offer the lowest prices in town.

Ex. from the film: But think of all the poor devils who can't *beat* Renaud's *price*.

**4. (to get/*have*) something ◆◆ to be preoccupied with something
   *on one's mind***

Definition: to be thinking about something seriously, to be considering something seriously

Ex. Friend to friend: I've *got something on my mind* and I need to talk to you confidentially about it.

Ex. from the film: Louis you *got something on your mind?*

5. (*as a*) *matter of fact* ◆◆ actually

Definition: just, only, actually
      This is often used to present conflicting evidence against a statement that has been made. It is often used to add evidence to an argument.

Ex. Man to woman: Would you like to go see that new horror movie that's in town?
      Woman to man: I don't really enjoy scary movies. *As a matter of fact*, I hate them.

Ex. from the film: *Matter of fact*, I wanted to give you a word of advice.

6. to *put* something *on one's bill* ◆→ to agree to pay for something in the future

Definition: to agree to pay for something, usually in a restaurant, often for other people

Ex. Three friends are in a bar. One friend says to the waiter: Can we have another pitcher of beer, please? Just *put* it *on my bill.*

Ex. from the film: Oh no, Emil, please, a bottle of your best champagne and *put it on my bill.*

7. *can't get over* ◆→ to be very surprised at something

Definition: to be very surprised by something

Ex. Child to child: I *can't get over* how angry my mother was when I told her I failed the class.

Ex. from the film: I *can't get over* you two.

8. to *become human* ◆→ to seem friendly

Definition: to suddenly seem friendly when one is not normally friendly

Ex. Student to student: The teacher *became* quite *human* when I told her that I was not feeling well. She told me to go home and rest and she told me I could take the test another day.

Ex. from the film: Rick, you're *becoming* quite *human.*

9. (to *have*) a curfew ◆→ to be required to be inside at a certain time of night

Definition: A curfew is an hour, set by authorities, by which people must be inside and off the street. A curfew can be set by parents for children, or, in times of civil unrest, a curfew can be set by governmental authorities.

Ex. Teenager to friend: I have to go. I *have a* ten o'clock *curfew* and my parents will be very angry if I'm back late.

Ex. from the film: And we *have a curfew* in Casablanca.

10. to *overstay one's welcome* ◆→ to remain beyond an appropriate length of time

Definition: to stay too long; to stay beyond an acceptable length of time; to stay so long that one's hosts become bored

Ex. Man to friend: Last night my friend Tom dropped by for a visit, but he really *overstayed his welcome.* He didn't leave until 2 A.M. Now I am so tired I can't work.

Ex. from the film: I hope we didn't *overstay our welcome.*

Activity 2

Directions to the teacher:

Have students read the following sentences. Instruct them to try to rewrite the sentences, replacing the items in bold print with one of the idioms from the list in Activity 1.

Directions to the students:

Read the following sentences. Then, rewrite the sentences, replacing the items in bold text with idioms from Activity 1.

1. Sales manager for General Office Supplies to a team of employees:

   I am very upset. I've **been thinking about something very seriously** for the past few days. The sign in front of Acme Office Supplies says that **they offer prices lower than those of any other office supply company in town**. We must not let then become number one in the market. I want you to **gather all of our sales representatives** and have a meeting to tell them that we will always be willing to offer our customers the same price as Acme Office Supplies.

   _____

   _____

   _____

   _____

   _____

   _____

2. Assistant sales manager:

   I think the reason Acme is so successful is because they have the **good fortune** to be located right next to the business district. I don't think there is anything we can do to compete with them. Do you really think we can be successful against them?

   _____

   _____

3. Sales manager:

   Yes, **actually** I do. I think we need to plan hard and work together, but I think we can be successful against them.

   _____

Activity 3

Directions to the teacher:

Have the students work in pairs to complete the following dialogues, using at least one idiom from Activity 1. After you have checked their work, have them practice the dialogues with their partners.

Directions to the students:

Work with a partner to complete the following dialogues. Be sure to use at least one idiom from Activity 1 in each dialogue. After your teacher has checked your work, practice your dialogue with your partner.

1. Situation: In a restaurant. There is a group of six people.

   Waiter: Will there be anything else?

   Tom: _____

   _____

2. Situation: In a teacher's lounge at a school.

   First teacher: Well, I heard that my students had tests in three other classes today, so I post- poned the test I had planned.

   Second teacher: _____

   _____

3. Situation: At a police checkpoint on the highway.

   Police: No cars are allowed on the highway after ten p.m. There have been reports of dangerous flooding about ten miles further on.

   Motorist: _____

   _____

4. Situation: At the end of a party.

   Host: Oh please! Stay a few more minutes! It's such fun talking to you!

   Guest: _____

   _____

5. Situation: On a street corner.

   Woman: _____

   _____

   Man: Thank you. I've been dieting for two months. My wife is also very happy with the way I look.

Scene 1 The Refugee Trail

Teaching Point

English has different stress patterns for different types of words. For purposes of listening, it is often helpful to think in terms of **primary** and **secondary** stress. **Primary stress** is the strongest stress in a phrase.

In **adjective-noun phrases**, the noun gets the primary stress (•). Listen as your teacher says these phrases. Then, try repeating them, using the same stress pattern.

> •
> Second World War
>
> •
> imprisoned Europe
>
> •
> French Morocco

In **noun-noun phrases**, the stressed syllable of the first noun gets the primary stress. In these phrases, the first word is not always a noun. Sometimes, it is an adjective acting as a noun. Listen as your teacher says these phrases. Then, try repeating them, using the same stress pattern.

> •
> embarkation point
>
> •
> refugee trail
>
> •
> exit visas
>
> •
> New World

In **noun lists**, each noun gets the same primary stress. Listen as your teacher says this list. Then, try repeating it, using the same stress pattern.

> •   •   •
> by train, or auto, or foot
>
> •   •   •
> through money, or influence, or luck

Phrasal verbs are verbs followed by certain prepositions. Phrasal verbs have different meanings than the same verbs without prepositions. In phrasal verbs, the preposition gets the primary stress. Listen as your teacher says this phrasal verb. Then, try repeating it, using the same stress pattern.

> •
> sprang up = developed

Activity 1

Directions to the teacher:

Place the students in pairs. Show the entire first scene one time with the sound turned off. After the students have completed the activity, check for comprehension in a large group discussion.

Directions:

Work with another student. Look at this scene with the sound turned off. This scene has a *voice-over*; that is, a narrator reads a description of the scene and information about the movie. Try to imagine what the narrator is saying. With your partner, write a paragraph describing the scene. Then, read it to another pair of students. Compare your paragraphs.

Activity 2

Directions to the teacher:

Play the scene with the sound on from the point where the narrator says "With the coming..." to "... wait, and wait, and wait." Have the students work in pairs to fill in the cloze passage. Then, check for comprehension in a large group discussion.

Directions to the students:

In pairs, listen to the following passage. Write the words you hear in the spaces. After you have written your words, compare your work with that of your partner.

> With the coming of the _____ _____ _____, many eyes in _____ _____ turned hopefully, or desperately, toward the freedom of the Americas. Lisbon became the great _____ _____, but not everybody could get to Lisbon directly, and so a tortuous, roundabout _____ _____ _____ _____ –Paris to Marseille–across the Mediterranean to Oran–then by _____, or _____, or _____ across the rim of Africa–to Casablanca in _____ _____. Here the fortunate ones–through _____, or _____, or _____–might obtain _____ _____ and scurry to Lisbon, and from Lisbon to the _____ _____. But the others wait in Casablanca, and wait, and wait, and wait.

Activity 3

Directions to the teacher:

Maintain the pairings from the previous scene. Play the entire scene one time with the sound on. Have the students discuss the questions. Check for comprehension in a large group discussion.

Directions to the students:

With your partner, listen to the whole scene again. Then, answer these questions. Share your answers with the other students in your class.

1. Why do people go to Casablanca?
2. Where do people go after they leave Casablanca?
3. What do people need in order to leave Casablanca?

Scene 2   Police Question Suspects

Idiom in this scene

> round up

Activity 1

Directions to the teacher:

> *Place the students in pairs. Play the entire scene one time with the sound turned off. Have the students discuss the answer to the question.*

Directions to the students:

> With a partner, watch the entire scene with the sound turned off. Discuss the answer to this question:
>
>> Why did the policemen ask to see the man's papers?

Activity 2

Directions to the teacher:

> *Place the students in pairs. After the students are finished with the activity, check for comprehension in a large group discussion.*

Directions to the students:

> With a partner, classify the following words into the type of phrases that you learned about in Scene 1, Activity 2. Check your dictionary if you are unsure of the part of speech. Determine where the stress will fall. Practice saying them.
>
>> German couriers
>> important official documents
>> possible accomplices
>> round up
>> suspicious characters

Activity 3

Directions to the teacher:

> *Keep the students in pairs. Play the scene one time with the sound on from the words "to all officers..." until "Important." Have the students fill in the words and then share their work with their partners. Check for comprehension in a large group discussion.*

Directions to the students:

> In pairs, listen to the scene one time. Write the words you hear in the following passage. Discuss what you have written with your partner.

To all officers. _____ _____ _____ carrying _____

_____ _____ _____ on train from Oran.

_____ and _____ _____

headed for Casablanca. _____ _____ _____

_____ _____ and search them for _____

_____. Important.

Teaching Point

Sometimes, in headlines and news bulletins, the verb *be* is taken out in the passive and in *be + adjective*. For example, a news bulletin might announce:

Building sold to foreign investors. Lawyers tired of negotiating.

This actually means

The building was sold to foreign investors. The lawyers are tired of negotiating.

Activity 4

Directions to the teacher:

Maintain the pairs. You may wish to play the scene one more time with the sound on. After the activity, check for comprehension in a large group discussion.

Directions to the students:

With a partner, look at the news bulletin in Activity 3 and find two places where the verb "be" has been taken out.
Write the full sentences here:

1._____

2._____

Activity 5

Directions to the teacher:

Maintain the pairs. Play the entire scene once more with the sound on. After the activity, check for comprehension in a large group.º

Directions to the students:

With your partner, listen to and watch the entire scene again. Then, discuss the answer to this question.

Why did the police ask to see the man's papers?

Scene 3 Rick & Ugarte at Rick's

Idioms in this scene:

lucky break

beat (someone's) price

Activity 1

Directions to the teacher:

Divide the students into pairs of A and B. Follow these directions for a silent narration: Have student A face the video screen. Have student B sit next to student A but facing away from the video screen. Play the entire clip with the sound off.

Directions to student A:

You are going to watch a scene from the movie *Casablanca.* As you watch the scene you will tell your partner (student B) what is going on in the movie. Student B will not be able to see the movie and neither you nor student B will be able to hear the movie. Keep these important questions in mind as you are telling your partner the story:

1. What do you think the two men are talking about?
2. How do the two men feel about each other? How do you know?

It's important to speak clearly and to think about the grammar and vocabulary you will use. Before you begin watching, think about these questions:

1. What tense(s) should you use to describe actions that are happening as you are describing them?
2. How will you refer to people? For example, if there are two men, how will you refer to them so that your partner understands which one you are speaking about?

Directions to student B:

You are going to be told about a movie. You will not see the movie. Student A will tell you about the movie. Pay close attention.

Activity 2

Directions to the teacher:

Maintain the pairings. Play the entire scene one time with the sound turned on. Let the students discuss the answers to the questions. Check for comprehension in a large group discussion.

Directions to the students:

With your partner, view the entire scene one time with the sound turned on. As you listen, try to answer these questions. Discuss the answers to the questions when you have finished listening.

1. What are the two men talking about?
2. How do the two men feel about each other? How do you know?

Teaching Point

As you learned in the first chapter, some English questions show the feeling, the expectation, or the bias of the speaker. There are many different ways that speakers can show their attitudes and expectations by the way they forms questions.

Words can be used to show feeling.

Stress, especially unusually heavy stress on a certain word, can also show feeling or expectation.

Sometimes the grammar of a question, especially tag questions and negative questions, can convey attitude and feeling.

Sometimes the fact that a speaker even asks a question, especially when a question is not necessary, can show a feeling.

Activity 3 (Clip 3A)

Directions to the teacher:

Place the students in pairs. Play the scene two times from the point where Ugarte says "You know Rick, watching you..." to "today they're the honored dead." Have the students listen for the missing questions. Check for comprehension in a large group discussion.

Directions to the students:

With a partner, listen to the following clip. Write down all the questions that you hear. Share your answers with your partner.

Ugarte: You know, Rick, watching you just now with the Deutsche Bank, one would think you've been doing this all your life.

Rick: (1) _____?

Ugarte: Oh, nothing. But when you first came to Casablanca, I thought...

Rick: (2) _____?

Ugarte: (3) _____? (4) _____?
(5) _____?

Rick: They got a lucky break. Yesterday they were just two German clerks; today they're the honored dead.

With your partner, decide which features of each question show the speaker's attitude and what that attitude is.

Question 1: _____

Structure that shows attitude: _____

Attitude that it shows: _____

Question 2: _____

Structure that shows attitude: _____

Attitude that it shows: _____

Question 3: _____

Structure that shows attitude: _____

Attitude that it shows: _____

Question 4: _____

Structure that shows attitude: _____

Attitude that it shows: _____

Question 5: _____

Structure that shows attitude: _____

Attitude that it shows: _____

Teaching Point

One way that a speaker can make a polite, negative sentence is to use the **unreal conditional** to state a condition that is not true with a different outcome.

For example, a person can say:

If I ever went to bed before ten, I might feel well rested.

This is a nice way of saying:

I don't go to bed early and I don't feel well rested.

Activity 4 (Clip 3B)

Directions to the teacher:

Maintain the pairs. Play the scene twice with the sound on, from the point where Ugarte says "You are a very cynical person…" to the point where Rick says "Well,…" Have the students fill in the missing parts and compare notes. Check for comprehension in a large group discussion.

Directions to the students:

You will hear the following dialogue clip twice. Work with a partner and listen for the questions and the unreal conditional. Write them in the spaces shown. Share your answers with your partner.

Ugarte: You are a very cynical person, Rick, if you'll forgive me for saying so.

Rick: I'll forgive you.

Ugarte: Thank you. (1) _____?

Rick: No.

Ugarte: Oh, I forgot you never drink with any… I'll have another, please.

Waiter: Yes, monsieur.

Ugarte: (2) _____?

Rick: Well, (3) _____.

With your partner, answer the following questions about the questions you wrote.

Question 1: _____

Structure that shows attitude: _____

Attitude that it shows: _____

Question 2: _____

Structure that shows attitude: _____

Attitude that it shows: _____

Question 3: _____

Structure that shows attitude: _____

Attitude that it shows about how Rick feels towards Ugarte:

_____

Activity 5 (Clip 3C)

Directions to the teacher:

> *Place the students in small groups. Show the clip twice with the sound on from the point where Ugarte says "But why?" to where he says "I found myself much more reasonable." Have the students discuss the answers to the questions. Check for comprehension in a large group discussion.*

Directions to the students:

In small groups, look up the words *parasite* and *parasitic* in the dictionary. Then, listen to the clip twice. Discuss the answers to these questions.

1. What is Ugarte's profession?
2. Who else is in the same business?
3. How is Ugarte "parasitic"?

Activity 6 (Clip 3D)

Directions to the teacher:

> *Place the students in small groups. Show the clip twice with the sound on from the point where Ugarte says "Look, Rick" to where he says "I knew I could trust you." Have the students discuss the answers to the questions. Check for comprehension in a large group discussion.*

Directions:

In small groups, listen to the clip twice. Discuss the answers to the questions.

1. What does Ugarte have?
2. Where do you think Ugarte got what he has? (This question will require you to think carefully about what you have learned in previous clips.)
3. What is Ugarte going to do tonight?
4. What does Ugarte want Rick to do for him?

Activity 7 (Clip 3E)

Directions to the teacher:

> *Play the clip twice with the sound on from the point where Ugarte says "Waiter!" until the end of the clip. Have the students discuss the answers to the questions in small groups. Check for comprehension in a large group discussion.*

Directions to the students:

> In small groups, listen carefully to the following clip and then, using everything you have learned in all three clips you have done so far, answer the following questions:
>
> 1. Why is Rick impressed with Ugarte?
> 2. What can you guess about Rick's political beliefs?

Scene 4 Rick & Louis in Rick's Office

Idioms in this scene:

> to have something on (one's) mind
>
> as a matter of fact

Activity 1

Directions to the teacher:

> *Have students use their English-English dictionaries to look up the following idioms. You may wish to help them by pointing out which key word will help them find the idioms in their dictionaries.*

Directions to the students:

> Use your English-English dictionaries to look up the following idioms.
>
> 1. a word of advice
>   meaning: _____
>
> 2. permit (someone) to (do something)
>   meaning: _____
>
> 3. let (someone) (do something)
>   meaning: _____
>
> 4. impress half the world
>   meaning: _____
>
> 5. spill (something)
>   meaning: _____

Activity 2 (Clip 4A)

Directions to the teacher:

Place the students in triads. Show the students the scene from the beginning, where Rick says, "Louis you got something on your mind" to the point where Louis says, "He stays in Casablanca." Show it two times with the sound on. Have them fill in the blanks in the dialogue and share their answers. Check for comprehension in a large group discussion.

Directions to the students:

In groups of three, watch the section of the video which your teacher will play for you and fill in the missing words. Share your answers with each other.

Rick: Louis you _____ something on your _____. Why don't you _____ __?

Louis: How observant you are. Matter of fact I wanted to give you __ _____ __ _____.

Rick: Yeah, brandy?

Louis: Thank you. Rick, there are many _____ _____ sold in this cafe but we know that you've never sold one. That is the reason we _____ you to _____ open.

Rick: I thought it was because I _____ you win at roulette.

Louis: That is another reason. There is a man arrived in Casablanca on his way to America. He will offer a fortune to anyone who will furnish him with an _____ _____.

Rick: What's his name?

Louis: Victor Laslo.

Rick: Victor Laslo!

Louis: Rick, that is the first time I have ever seen you so impressed.

Rick: Well, he's succeeded in _____ half the world.

Louis: It's my duty to see that he doesn't impress the other _____. Rick, Laslo must never reach America. He stays in Casablanca.

Teaching Point

People use **formal** or **informal speech** for different reasons. One reason is to show their personalities. Some people prefer to project an informal, relaxed attitude. Other people prefer to project a formal, serious attitude. Of course, the same person may use informal speech in one setting or situation and formal speech in another setting or situation.

Example: **Come off it!** (informal)
You're not really serious? (formal)
(Both show disbelief.)

Example: **Nice to meet you.** (informal)
It's a great pleasure to meet you. (formal)
(Both are used when meeting someone.)

Activity 3 (Clip 4A)

Directions to the teacher:

Have students work in pairs or small groups to characterize the language from the clip. Then have them answer the questions that follow.

Directions to the students:

Put a check in either the *formal* or *informal* blank next to each statement.

	Informal	Formal
1. Why don't you spill it?	_____	_____
2. How observant you are.	_____	_____
3. Yeah, brandy?	_____	_____
4. We permit you to remain open.	_____	_____
5. I let you win at roulette.	_____	_____

Now answer these questions.

1. Who is using informal language in this scene?

2. Who is using formal language in this scene?

3. Why is one man using formal language and the other using informal language?

Activity 4 (clip 4A)

Directions to the teacher:

Place the students in pairs. Show the students the scene from the point where Rick says, "What's his name?" to the point where Rick says, "Victor Laslo!" Show it two times with the sound on. Have the students discuss the questions and then check for comprehension in a large group discussion.

Directions to the students:

In pairs, watch the section of the video which your teacher will play for you and answer the following questions.

1. Describe the way Louis says, "Victor Laslo."

2. Describe the way Rick says, "Victor Laslo!"

3. Are both men impressed with Victor Laslo?

4. Which half of the world has Victor Laslo impressed? What do you think he might have done to impress it?

Now, work with a partner to try to repeat the lines in the same way that Rick and Louis say them.

Rick: What's his name?

Louis: Victor Laslo.

Rick: Victor Laslo!

Now work with a partner using the same intonation pattern with different names in the following dialogue.

A: I met a famous person last night.

B: Who was it?

A: _____.*

B: _____!

*Suggestions:

Prince Charles	Mick Jagger
Madonna	Princess Diana
Michael Jackson	Boris Yeltsin

Teaching Points

Another form of **clarification question** uses a verb followed by a question word to ask for more information. This is often the case when the object of the verb has been deleted. Consider the following example:

A: She often refuses.

B: Refuses what?

A: Refuses to date him.

Betting and the use of **betting language** is common in English. A common expression is "Bet you" (pronounced "becha") to mean "I am sure that…" For example, one could say: "I becha didn't know that they got divorced" to mean "I am sure that you didn't know that they got divorced."

Betting for money is also common. There are several ways to make a bet in English. The most common is to say:
"I bet five dollars that the Dodgers do/don't win the game."

The common responses would be:
"You're on."
"I'll take that bet."
"O.K."

to show acceptance of the bet or
"No bet."
"Not on your life"
"No way."

to show a rejection of the bet.

Activity 5 (Clip 4B)

Directions to the teacher:

> *Place the students in small groups. Show the part of the scene from the point where Rick says, "It'll be interesting to see how he manages" to the point where Louis says, "There is no exit visa for him." Play it two or more times with the sound on. Have the students answer the following questions. Check for comprehension in a large group discussion.*

Directions to the students:

In small groups, watch the part of the scene that the teacher plays for you. Answer the following questions.

1. What does Rick think Laslo will manage?

   _____

2. How does Rick offer to bet? (write the words)

   _____

   _____

3. How does Louis change the bet? (write the words)

   _____

   _____

4. What are they betting about?

   _____

   _____

Teaching Point

Every language has ways for people to make a point. A very common way in English is to make a general point with an opinion and then provide evidence to support the point. Consider the following example:

He was really a wonderful husband. He helped his wife through childbirth, and after the baby was born he volunteered to stay home and take care of the baby since his wife wanted to resume her career.

The first sentence–He was really a wonderful husband–is a general opinion. The evidence to support the opinion is that he helped his wife through childbirth and stayed home to take care of the baby.

Activity 6 (Clip 4C)

Directions to the teacher:

Have the students look up the words below in their English-English dictionaries before listening to the clip. Place the students in triads. Play the clip twice with the sound on from where Rick says "Louis whatever gave you…" to the point where Rick says "Maybe." Have the students answer the questions. Check for comprehension in a large group discussion.

Directions to the students:

Look up the following two words below in your English-English dictionary. Then, in small groups listen to the clip two times. After that, work with the others in your group to answer the questions.

1. cynical_____

2. sentimentalist _____

Now discuss the answers to these questions:

1. What general opinion does Louis have about Rick?

2. What evidence does Louis offer to support his opinion?

   In 1935 _____

   In 1936 _____

   Both groups _____

3. What does Louis think Rick might do?

4. Do you think Rick might help Laslo? Why or why not?

Scene 5 Laslo, Ilse & Rick at a Table in Rick's

Idiom in this scene:

> to put it on (one's) bill

Activity 1

Directions to the teacher:

> *Place the students in pairs. Play the entire scene for the students and ask them to identify the people in the scene and the people who are talked about in the scene. Check for comprehension in a large group discussion.*

Directions to the students:

In pairs, watch the scene your teacher will play for you. Then, try to identify the people in the scene and the people who are talked about in the scene. Share your answers with your partner.

Draw lines from the names of the characters to the appropriate category.

Rick

Victor Laslo   in this scene

Ilse Lunt   mentioned in this scene

Sam

Louis Renaud

Now write the occupation of each person.

Rick   _____

Victor Laslo   _____

Ilse Lunt   _____

Sam   _____

Louis Renaud   _____

Activity 2

Directions to the teacher:

Place the students in triads. Play the section of the scene beginning when Louis says, "I am Captain Renaud. Prefect of Police." through the point where Laslo says, "Won't you join us?" Play it at least twice with the sound on. Have the students characterize the tone of each statement that has a parenthesis next to it. Have them discuss their answers and check for comprehension in a large group discussion.

Directions to the students:

In small groups, watch the section of the video that your teacher will play for your. As you watch it, try to characterize the remarks of Louis and Victor Laslo. Share your answers with the members of your group.

To characterize their remarks, use the following words:

COLDER				WARMER
I_____	I_____	I_____	I_____	I
cold	cool	neutral	pleasant	warm

Louis: Mssr. Laslo is it not?

Laslo: Yes.

Louis: I am Captain Renaud. Prefect of Police.

Laslo: Yes, what is it you want?   (_____)

Louis: Merely to welcome you to Casablanca and   (_____)
to wish you a pleasant stay. It isn't often
we have so distinguished a visitor.

Laslo: Thank you. I hope you will forgive me   (_____)
Captain. The present French administration
hasn't always been so cordial. May I
present Miss Ilse Lund?

Louis: I was informed you were the most   (_____)
beautiful woman ever to visit Casablanca.
That was a gross understatement.

Ilse: You are very kind.

Laslo: Won't you join us?

Now answer these questions:

1. Whose tone was friendlier? How did you decide?

2. Whose tone was colder? How did you decide?

Teaching Point

We sometimes use **cold formality**, as Victor Laslo did, to show that we don't feel friendly towards the person to whom we are talking. In order to do this, we must first identify the formal alternatives to everyday expressions.

Example: That's great.   **How nice for you.**
                (informal)   **(formal)**

Activity 3

Directions to the teacher:

Place the students in pairs. Have the students match up the informal and formal expressions with the same meaning. Then, have them practice the situational dialogues which follow.

Directions to the students:

Draw lines between the formal and informal expressions in the following columns. Then, complete the situational dialogues and practice them with a partner.

Informal	Formal
Nice to meet you.	How well you look, considering.
That's a nice dress.	Won't you take a seat.
You look great.	How nice to meet you.
Please have a seat.	What an interesting outfit.

Now, fill in the correct cold response for each situation.

1. Situation: Someone you don't like asks to join you at a party.

   Other person: Hi! Nice evening! May I join you?

   You: _____

2. Someone approaches you at a party. The person is drunk and obnoxious. The person is bragging about how great he or she feels.

   Other person: Boy, I feel great! You know, I've been working out for about six months now and it's really made a difference.

   You: _____

Now practice these dialogues with a partner.

Teaching Point

Sometimes it's easier to describe someone by saying what he or she is like, often in an **adjective clause**, rather than by using one or two words. Sometimes, in conversation, we use a **conditional** to express the idea as well. This form is used only in conversation.

> **Example: She's the kind of person who would do anything for you.**
> **(She's very generous.)**

> **Example: He's the kind of guy– if you invited him home, your parents would get really upset.**
> **(He's not wholesome.)**

Activity 4

Directions to the teacher:

> *Place the students in pairs. Show the students the part of the scene beginning where Ilse says, "Rick? Who's he?" through the point where Louis says, "Oh, excuse me." Play the scene two times with the sound on. Ask the students to work together in pairs to answer the following questions. Check for comprehension in a large group discussion.*

Directions to the students:

Watch the part of the scene that your teacher will show you. Then, work with a partner to answer these questions:

1. What does Ilse want to know about Rick?

2. How does Louis describe Rick?

3. Is Louis' description of Rick positive?

Now, try to describe someone you know, whom your partner doesn't know. Use an adjective clause or a conditional.

You: I just had a letter from _____.

Partner: _____. Who's he/she?

You: He/she's my _____ from _____.

Partner: What's he/she like?

You: He/she's the kind of person _____

_____.

Practice the dialogue with your partner.

Scene 6 Rick & Ilse Meet Again

Idioms in this scene:

>   can't get over
>   to become human
>   to have a curfew
>   to overstay (one's) welcome

Activity 1

Directions to the teacher:

> *Have the students use their English-English dictionaries to look up the following words.*

Directions to the students:

Use your English-English dictionaries to look up these words:

>   1. hear a great deal about
>   meaning: _____
>
>   2. precedent
>   meaning: _____
>
>   3. congratulate
>   meaning: _____
>
>   4. (one's) work
>   meaning: _____

Activity 2

Directions to the teacher:

Place the students in triads. Play the scene from the point where Laslo says, "One hears a great deal about Rick in Casablanca" through the point where Rick says, "We all try. You succeed." Play it two times. Then have the students answer the following questions. Check for comprehension in a large group discussion.

Directions to the students:

In small groups of three, watch the scene which your teacher will play for you. Then answer the following questions with the members of your group.

1. What words does Laslo use to congratulate Rick?

   _____

2. What does Laslo congratulate Rick about?

   _____

3. What words does Rick use to congratulate Laslo?

   _____

4. What does Rick congratulate Laslo about?

   _____

5. Why is Louis surprised?

   _____

Activity 3

Directions to the teacher:

Play the part of the scene beginning where Ilse says, "I wasn't sure you were the same" through the point where Ilse says, "When the Germans march out, I'll wear it again." Place the students in small groups. Have the students read along with the dialogue and focus on Rick's speech. Have the students answer the following questions. Then, check for comprehension in a large group discussion.

Directions to the students:

In small groups, watch the scene that your teacher will play for you. Follow along with the printed dialogue that follows. Concentrate on what Rick says. Then, answer the following questions. Share your answers with the members of your group .

Ilse: I wasn't sure you were the same. Let's see the last time we met....

Rick: Was the Belle Aurora.

Ilse: How nice. You remembered. But of course that was the day the Germans marched into Paris.

Rick: Not an easy day to forget.

Ilse: No.

Rick: I remember every detail. The Germans wore grey. You wore blue.

Ilse: Yes. I put that dress away. When the Germans march out, I'll wear it again.

Now, answer these questions:

1. How does Rick's reaction to Ilse seem to you?

2. What seems wrong about Rick's line, "I remember every detail. The Germans wore grey. You wore blue"? What comparison is he making between Ilse and the Germans?

3. What tone do you think Rick is taking?

4. Why do you think he is taking that tone?

Activity 4

Directions to the teacher:

Place the students in small groups. Play the last part of the scene from the point where Laslo says, "We'll come again" to the point where Rick says, "He hasn't played it in a long time." Have the students answer the following questions. Check for comprehension in a large group discussion.

Directions to the students:

In small groups, watch the last part of the scene that your teacher will play for you. Then, answer the following questions. Share your answers with the members of your group.

1. How do you know that Rick and Ilse knew each other before?

2. What do you think is the significance of the song "As Time Goes By"?

3. Why do you think Sam hasn't played that song in a long time?

Pre-Viewing Questions

1. A love triangle is a standard convention of Hollywood movies. Do you think there is a love triangle in Casablanca? What people are at each point of the triangle?

2. There are two central issues in this movie. One is personal. The other is political. What do you think these issues are? How do you think they will turn out?

   Personal issue: _____

   Political issue: _____

3. What is the difference between a cynic and a romantic? Who do you think is a cynic in this movie? Who do you think is a romantic?

Post-Viewing Questions

1. What were the two major, conflicting problems that Rick faced? How did he resolve them?

2. What were the personal and political issue in this movie? How did they connect?

3. What would you have done if you had been Rick?

4. What would you have done if you had been Ilse?

Post-Viewing Activities

1. Read the book *Voyage of the Damned* which is about a group of Jews who tried to escape from the Nazis. Divide the book into sections and have each student report on the section he/she read.

2. *Casablanca* is a film that has been copied by many different directors. Watch one of the following movies and explain to the members of your class how the director copies the *Casablanca* story:

   > *Play it Again Sam*
   > *Havana*
   > *Tequila Sunrise*

3. Read the book *The Winds of War* and the follow-up book *War and Remembrance* by Herman Wouk. These are long books and you may want to divide them up among the members of your class.

If You Liked This Film

You may wish to see these films about escapes from Nazi aggression:

Julia (1977) starring Vanessa Redgrave and Jane Fonda. Directed by Fred Zinnemann (118 min. color).

The Winds of War (miniseries) (1983) starring Robert Mitchum and Ali McGraw (color).

The Eye of the Needle (1981) starring Donald Sutherland and Kate Nelligan. Directed by Richard Marquand (112 min. color).

Foreign Correspondent (1940) starring Joel McCrea and Laraine Day. Directed by Alfred Hitchcock (119 min. black and white).

Chapter 5

Laimute E. Druskis

Ted Poweski

Ken Karp

As You Begin

Directions:

Read the following short passage. Look at the pictures. Then, in groups of three or four, discuss the questions.

In most languages, the way women and men speak is different. Some choices in speech style are individual, but it is generally accepted that there is a "normal" range within which women can operate without being "different," and there is a "normal" range within which men can operate without being "different." The question of how society assigns "appropriate" language to each sex has been under serious study for some time. The basic question is: How are people restricted in expressing themselves by the sex-based language rules of society?

1. Think about your native language. Do men and women use the language differently?

2. What are some of the features of women's speech in your language (including both verbal and nonverbal language)?

3. What are some of the features of men's speech in your language (including both verbal and nonverbal language)?

4. What have you observed about the differences in men's and women's speech in English?

A Reading to Get Things Started

Directions:

Read the following passage. Use your dictionary to find words that you don't know. After you have finished reading, discuss the answers to the questions with a classmate or a small group of your classmates.

Vocabulary List

Metamessages – Features of conversation, including word choice, intonation choice, and body language, that a speaker uses to communicate his or her message.

Framing

Another way to think about **metamessages** is that they *frame* a conversation, much as a picture frame provides a context for the images in the picture. Metamessages let you know how to interpret what someone is saying by identifying the activity that is going on: Is this an argument or a chat? Is it helping, advising, or scolding? At the same time, they let you know what position the speaker is assuming in the activity, and what position you are being assigned.

Sociologist Erving Goffman uses the term alignment to express this aspect of framing. If you put me down, you are taking a superior alignment with respect to me. Furthermore, by showing the alignment that you take with regard to others, what you say frames you, just as you are framing what you say. For example, if you talk to others as if you were a teacher and they were your students, they may perceive that your way of talking frames you as condescending or pedantic. If you talk to others as if you were a student seeking help and explanations, they may think of you as insecure, incompetent, or naive. Our reactions to what others say or do are often sparked by how we feel we are being framed.

From *You Just Don't Understand* by Deborah Tannen, Ph.D.© 1990 by Deborah Tannen, Ph.D. By permission of William Morrow, Inc..

Questions for Discussion

1. What does Dr. Tannen mean by "framing"?

2. Dr. Tannen gives examples of several frames: an argument, a chat, helping, advising, scolding. Give examples of some other frames.

3. Give another example of putting yourself in superior alignment with regard to someone else.

4. Give an example of a comfortable frame in which someone else put you.

5. Give an example of a uncomfortable frame in which someone else put you.

6. You are going to an embassy to get a visa. In what frame would you put yourself? In what frame would you put the embassy personnel?

Idioms from the Film, *When Harry Met Sally*

Directions to the teacher:

> *Read the following list of idioms and have students repeat them for correct pronunciation.*

Activity 1

Directions to the students:

Listen as your teacher reads the following list of idioms. Pay attention to the teacher's pronunciation. Then study the list. These idioms are from the video scenes you will be working with.

1. (have/got) *to catch a plane* ◆→ **to board a plane**

Definition: to get on a plane; to arrive at a plane in time to fly somewhere

Example: Executive to secretary: Tell Ms. Smith to call back on Monday. I have to go now. I have *to catch a plane.*

Example from the film: Well, listen, I got *a plane to catch.*

---

*Language note: When "to catch a plane" is preceded by **have/got**, the infinitive **to catch** can be placed after **plane**, as in this example. Additionally, other types of motorized transportation can be substituted for "plane": I have to catch a cab and go downtown.*

---

2. *to place* **(someone)** ◆→ **to remember (someone)**

Definition: To remember someone from the past, especially someone who has not been seen in a long time. This is used particularly when someone must think very hard to remember.

Example: Husband to wife: Last night at the party, I met a man who said he had gone to college with me. I thought about it for a while, but I just couldn't *place him.*

Example from the film: Thank God he couldn't *place me.*

Language note: This is usually used in the negative when someone fails to remember someone.

---

3. *to make a pass at* **(someone)** ◆→ **to proposition (someone)**

Definition: to make a sexual advance towards someone; to ask someone, usually indirectly, if she or he would like to have sex

Example: One woman to another: I avoid going to bars by myself because I don't like it when men *make passes at me.*

Example from the film: He *made a pass at me,* and when I said no...

4. *to get involved with* **(someone)** ◆→ **to get into a romantic/sexual relationship with (someone)**

Definition: to arrive at a serious point in a romantic or sexual relationship

Example: One friend to another: When I was in college, I *got involved with* the woman who lived down the hall from me in the dormitory.

Example from the film: Don't *get involved with me,* Joe...

5. *to fall in love* **with (someone) ◆→ to have a romantic feeling towards (someone)**

Definition: to be in love with someone; to love someone in a romantic, though not necessarily sexual, way

Example: Woman to friend: I *fell in love with* my husband in college, but we didn't get involved until after we graduated.

Example from the film: And they *fall* madly *in love*.

Language note: This idiom focuses on the feeling of love. Idiom 4, to get involved with someone, focuses on the actual relationship.

---

6. *to be with* **(someone) ◆→ to be in a sexual or romantic relationship with (someone)**

Definition: to be involved with someone in a sexual or romantic way

Example: Man to friend: When I *was with* Julia in college, we were very compatible.

Example from the film: You*'re* not *with* Joe anymore?

Language note: This idiom is used mainly in referring to sexual relationships outside of marriage.

---

7. *to break up* **◆→ to end a romantic or sexual relationship; to divorce; to separate.**

Definition: to end a romantic or sexual relationship; to divorce, to separate

Example: Woman to friend: When my ex-husband and I *broke up*, we divided the property evenly between us.

Example from the film: We just *broke up*.

8. *to come down with* **something ◆→ to get sick with the flu or a cold**

Definition: to be at the beginning stages of a cold or flu, when the first symptoms are felt

Example: Child to teacher: I just sneezed three times. I think I'm *coming down with* something.

Example from the film: Maybe I'm *coming down with* something.

9. (food) *on the side* **◆→ sauce or food served with other food**

Definition: Food that accompanies other food and is served at the same time, but does not touch the main food that it accompanies. In this way, the person who eats the food must mix them together as she or he wishes.

Example: Man to waiter: I'd like the pie with ice cream, but please put the ice cream *on the side*.

Example from the film: Waiter, I'll begin with the house salad, but I don't want the regular dressing. I'll have the balsamic vinegar and oil, but on the side, and then the salmon with the mustard sauce, but I want the mustard sauce *on the side*.

10. *to go around* ♦♦ **(for a disease) to spread**

Definition: For a disease to spread. This is usually used to refer to relatively less serious diseases, such as flu and colds.

Example: Doctor to 80-year old patient: There is a flu *going around*. You need to be careful.

Example from the film: I'm definitely coming down with something. Probably a twenty-four-hour tumor. They're *going around*.

Activity 2

Directions to the teacher:

Have students read the following sentences. Instruct them to rewrite the sentences replacing the items in bold print with one of the idioms from the list in Activity 1.

Directions to the students:

Read the following sentences. Then rewrite the sentences, replacing the items in bold text with idioms from Activity 1.

1. You know, the other day that guy Joe who's in my chemistry class invited me to dinner. After dinner, while we were paying the bill, he **suggested that it would be nice to stay at the hotel together**.

   What did you say?

   _____

   _____

   _____

   _____

2. I said I had no interest in **starting any kind of romantic relationship with him** and that I just wanted to be friends.

   What did he say to that?

   _____

   _____

   _____

   _____

3. He told me that **he had been living with** a woman for the last five years and that **recently their relationship had ended.** He apologized and told me that he was just starting to date again and that he really didn't know how to talk to women. He agreed it would be a good idea just to be friends. Besides, it is just not safe to sleep with strangers. There are all kinds of diseases **that you can catch!** He agreed. He told me that one of his friends died recently from AIDS.

   _____

   _____

   _____

   _____

Activity 3

Directions to the teacher:

Have the students work in pairs to complete the following dialogues using at least one idiom from Activity 1. After you have checked their work, have them practice the dialogues with their partners.

Directions to the students:

Work with a partner to complete the following dialogues. Be sure to use at least one idiom from Activity 1 in each dialogue. After your teacher has checked your work, practice your dialogue with your partner.

1. Situation: In a pharmacy.

   Man: _____

   Druggist: Well, it sounds like you may have the flu. Maybe you should see the doctor before taking any medicine.

2. Situation: At a party.

   Woman: Hi Joe! It's certainly been a long time since I've seen you.

   Joe: _____

   _____

3. Situation: At a marriage counselor's office.

   Man: _____

   _____

   Counselor: Well, if you don't want the marriage to end, you should explain your reasons to your wife.

4. Situation: Over a candle-lit dinner at a restaurant.

   Woman: _____

   _____

   Man: Well, I knew I loved you the first time I ever saw you.

5. Situation: On a busy corner in downtown Los Angeles.

   Woman: Oh hi Jill! How's it going?

   Jill: _____

   _____

Scene 1 Harry Meets Sally

Photofest

Activity 1

Directions to the teacher:

> *Put the students in small groups. Have them discuss the questions. Then, discuss the answers in a large group.*

Directions to the students:

In small groups, discuss the following questions:

1. How do men and women show romantic love in public in your country? What kinds of behavior are socially acceptable? Which are not?

2. How do you react when you see something that embarrasses you? How do people in your country react when they see something embarrassing?

3. Describe to other members of your group an embarrassing incident that you have witnessed. Explain your reaction to what you saw.

Activity 2

Directions to the teacher:

> *Place the students in groups of three. Assign one student in each group to be Harry, one to be Sally (the blonde), and the third to be Amanda (the dark-haired girl). Have the groups watch the scene three times with the sound off. Stop the tape after each watching and have the students write a script for the scene. With more mature students these scripts can be playacted.*

Directions to the students:

In groups of three, you will watch the scene three times with the sound off. One student in each group will write the part of Harry, one will write the part of Sally (the blonde), and the third will write the part of Amanda (the dark-haired girl). Try to write words that would be appropriate to the actions of the characters. Practice your script and be ready to perform it.

Amanda: _____

Harry: _____

Sally: _____

Harry: _____

Sally: _____

Amanda: _____

Harry: _____

Amanda: _____

Harry: _____

Amanda: _____

Harry: _____

Sally: _____

Harry: _____

Amanda: _____

Harry: _____

Activity 3

Directions to the teacher:

Keep the students in groups of three. Play the scene one time with the sound on.
Have the students discuss the answers to the questions. Check for comprehension in a
large group discussion.

Directions to the students:

In groups of three, listen to the scene one time. Discuss the answers to the
questions.

1. What happened when Harry met Sally?

2. Where are Harry and Sally going? What are they going to do?

3. What kind of person do you think Harry is? Why?

4. What kind of person do you think Sally is? Why?

Scene 2 On the way to New York

Teaching Point

One way to show preference between two choices is to use **would
rather**. Consider the following examples. Have your teacher say these
sentences. Notice the direction of the voice. The voice rises on the first choice
and drops on the second choice in the question. In the statement, the voice
drops on both choices.

↗   ↘

Would you rather have coffee or tea?

↘   ↘

I'd rather have coffee than tea.

Activity 1

Directions to the teacher:

Pair the students. Have one student ask the other a "would rather" question with two of the items in the list that follows the example. Have the other student answer with a "would rather" statement. Then, have the students discuss the reasons for their preferences After that, discuss the answers in a large group.

Directions to the students:

In pairs, discuss the following questions. One student should ask a "would rather" question with two of the items from the list and the other student should answer with a "would rather" statement.

> Example: Student A: **Would you rather marry a person with a similar ethnic background or with a similar educational background?**
>
> Student B: **I would rather marry a person with a similar ethnic background than a person with a similar educational background.**

Every person has his or her own ideas about what is important in a marriage partner. This is a list of ten possible characteristics. Maybe you can think of some others. When you've finished asking "would rather" questions, rank them in order of importance and discuss your ranking with the members of your group. Why are these characteristics important or unimportant for you?

1. A partner with whom you have romantic passion.
2. A partner who has a prestigious job or title.
3. A partner with whom you have a great sexual relationship.
4. A partner who shares your religious beliefs.
5. A partner who has a similar ethnic background.
6. A partner who has a similar educational background.
7. A partner with whom you share similar hobbies and interests.
8. A partner who has a certain physical type.
9. A partner who has a similar employment history.
10. A partner who has a healthy bank account.

Activity 2

Directions to the teacher:

Pair the students and have them look up the idiom "in one's right mind" and write and perform a brief role-play in which they use the word.

Directions to the students:

In pairs, look up the idiom "in one's right mind" and write a brief role-play in which you use the word. Perform your role-play in front of your class.

Activity 3

Directions to the teacher:

Put the students in groups of four. Have them listen to the scene two times and discuss the answers to the following questions. Check for comprehension in a large group discussion.

Directions to students:

In groups of four, watch the scene two times and discuss the answers to the following questions:

1. What are Harry and Sally arguing about?

2. What movie is the subject of the conversation?

3. According to Sally, what do women prefer in a relationship? What example does she give from the movie?

4. According to Harry, what do women prefer in a relationship? How is Harry's interpretation of the movie different from Sally's?

5. According to Harry, why does Sally not share his interpretation of the movie?

Teaching Point

There are many different ways to **express disagreement** in English. This scene illustrates three very common ways:

1. Simply tell the other person directly that he or she is wrong.

2. Frame a question in such a way that you expect a certain answer, so that the other person is almost forced to agree.

3. Present as much evidence as you can to support your side of the argument.

Activity 4

Directions to the teacher:

Pair the students. One student in each pair will be Harry, the other Sally. Play the scene two times. Each partner should listen for the three forms of disagreement in his or her person's speech. Check for comprehension in a large group discussion.

Directions to the students:

Get into pairs. Listen to the scene two times. One student should fill in the chart with Harry's words. The other student should fill in the chart with Sally's words. Compare your answers.

1. Harry's Part
Question that Harry frames to make Sally agree with him:

_____

_____

Evidence that Harry presents to prove his point:

_____

_____

_____

2. Sally's Part
Words that Sally uses to express simple disagreement:

_____

Evidence that Sally presents to prove her point:

_____

_____

_____

Activity 5

Directions to the teacher:

Pair the students and have them write and present role-plays in which they choose one of the following topics and disagree.

Directions to the students:

In pairs, choose one of the following topics. Then write, practice, and perform a role-play in which you disagree.

Topic 1. The earth is flat.

Topic 2. Nuclear bombs are necessary to keep peace.

Topic 3. Men should earn more than women

Scene 3   Sally & Joe at the Airport

Idioms in this scene:

(have/got) to catch a plane

to place (someone)

to make a pass at (someone)

to get involved with (someone)

Activity 1

Directions to the teacher:

Arrange the students in groups of four. Have them watch the scene one time with the sound off and then discuss the answers to the questions. Check for comprehension in a large group discussion.

Directions to the students:

In groups of four, watch the scene one time with the sound off and then discuss the answers to the questions.

1. Where does this scene take place?

2. How have Harry and Sally changed since the last scene?

3. What do you think Harry's reaction is on seeing Sally?

4. What do you think Sally's reaction is on seeing Harry?

Activity 2

Directions to the teacher:

Put the students in groups of five. Assign each student one of the parts of the conversation listed below. First, have the students listen to the scene one time up to the point where Harry walks away. Each student should listen for the signal words that indicate that the assigned part of the conversation is taking place. For example, the student who has the assignment "conversation closure" should listen for the words that signal that the conversation is closing and should write them down. Check for comprehension in large a group discussion.

Directions to the students:

In groups of five, listen for the words that signal the different parts of the conversation you are about to hear. Your teacher will assign you to listen for one part. Write the words in the space provided. Share your answers with the members of your group.

Reintroduction: _____

_____

General small talk: _____

_____

More serious talk
about current status: _____

_____

Introduction: _____

_____

Conversation
closure: _____

_____

Activity 3

Directions to the teacher:

Pair the students. Have them look up the following idioms, then write and perform a brief role-play in which they use the words.

Directions to the students:

Write a brief role-play in which you use the words. Perform your role-play in front of your class.

to place somebody

to make a pass at somebody

to go with somebody

to get involved with somebody

Activity 4

Directions to the teacher:

> Put the students in groups of four. Play the clip one time from the point at which Harry walks away until the point at which Sally says "Uh...I said..." Have the students discuss the answer to the following questions. Then, check for comprehension in a large group discussion.

Directions to the student:

> In groups of four, listen to the clip and discuss the answers to the following questions:

> Why do you think Sally tells her boyfriend all about her first meeting with Harry?

> Do you think Sally's boyfriend believes that men and women can be just friends?

Activity 5

Directions to the teacher:

> Put the students in groups of four. Play the entire clip one time through. Have the students discuss the answers to the following questions. Check for comprehension in large group discussion.

Directions to the students:

> In groups of four, listen to the clip one time and then discuss the answers to the following questions.

> 1. What kind of person do you think Harry has become?
> 2. What kind of person do you think Sally has become?
> 3. Which one do you think would make a better friend?
> 4. Do you think it is possible for men and women to be just friends? Why or why not?
> 5. Do you have any friends of the opposite sex? Is it common for people in your culture to do so?

Scene 4 In the Bookstore

Idioms in this scene:

to fall in love with (someone)

to be with (someone)

to break up

Activity 1

Directions to the teacher:

Place the students in pairs. Play the scene two times with the sound on. After the first viewing, have students circle the answers in the Yes/No column. After the second viewing, have them fill in the information in the "How Do You Know" column. Check for comprehension in a large group discussion.

Directions to the students:

In pairs, view the scene that your teacher will play for you. After the first viewing, circle the correct answers in the Yes/No column. After the second viewing, fill in the information in the "How Do You Know" column.

Question	Yes/No	How Do You Know?
1. Did Sally recognize Harry?	Yes No	_____ _____
2. Is Harry married?	Yes No	_____
3. Did Harry recognize Sally?	Yes No	_____ _____

Activity 2

Directions to the teacher:

Pair the students. One student should listen for Harry's words (questions 1 and 4). The other should listen for Sally's words (questions 2 and 3). Play the scene two times with the sound on. Have students write the dialogue to answer questions 1 through 4. Following this activity, discuss the answers to questions 5 and 6 with the students in a large group.

Directions to the students:

View the scene that your teacher will play for you. Write the dialogue that answers the questions 1 through 4. After you have finished, your teacher will discuss with you the answers to Question 5 and 6.

1. What question did Harry ask Sally about her love life?

_____

2. What answer did she give?

_____

3. What question did Sally ask Harry about his marriage?

_____

4. What answer did he give?

_____

5. What was the difference between the way Sally and Harry answered what was basically the same question? Think about what you have learned about the difference between men's and women's speech.

_____

6. Aside from being polite, why did Harry and Sally ask each other about their romantic relationships?

_____

Teaching Point

Much of the meaning of what someone says is carried in the way they say things and by the ideas they put together in conversation.

In this scene, Sally's friend and Sally add meaning to the what they say in three ways.

1. Asking a nonstandard question to get confirmation.

> **Example: You like him?** (Note the stress on "like." If this stress were on "him," the meaning would more likely be disbelief.)
>
> **You'd like to meet him?**

2. Putting two ideas together to show a result-reason relationship.

RESULT **REASON**

Relax. **It's a holiday. (That is, because it's a holiday, you should relax.)**

RESULT **REASON**

They'll get along. **They both like baseball.**

3. Implying some action that should be taken using a sentence fragment beginning with *so*.

> **So you've finished school.** (Implying that now you'll be looking for a job.)
>
> **So you broke up with Bill.** (Implying that you may be looking for another boyfriend.)

Activity 3 (Clip 4A)

Directions to the teacher:

Put the students in small groups. Show the first part of the scene, with the sound on, from the point where Sally's friend says, "Someone is staring at you in Personal Growth" through the point where Sally says, "Also he's obnoxious." Have the students fill in the blank lines. Then have them answer the questions that use the techniques described in the previous teaching point. Check for comprehension in a large group discussion.

Directions to the students:

In small groups, view the part of the scene that your teacher will show you. Fill in the missing words. After watching the video, copy the line that uses each of the techniques listed in the Teaching Point, state the implication of that line and the technique it represents. Discuss the question at the end of the activity.

Marie: Someone is staring at you in Personal Growth.

Sally: I know him. _____

Marie: Who is he?

Sally: Harry Burns. He's a political consultant.

Marie: He's cute.

Sally: _____

Marie: How do you know he's married?

Sally: Cause the last time I saw him, he was getting married.

Marie: When was that?

Sally: Six years ago.

Marie: _____

Sally: Also he's obnoxious.

What does each of the three lines imply? What technique is being used?

1. Line: _____

   Implication: _____

   Technique: _____

2. Line: _____

   Implication: _____

   Technique: _____

3. Line: _____

   Implication: _____

   Technique: _____

Activity 4

Directions to the teacher:

> *Have students form pairs or small groups. Ask them to write sentences based on the situations described next using the techniques from the teaching point in Activity 2.*

Directions to the students:

Work in pairs or small groups to write sentences for the situations described next. Use the techniques from the Activity 2.

1. You think your friend is tired because she works too hard. What will you say to her?

   _____

2. Your sister just told you that she's thinking of marrying her boyfriend, Bob. You like Bob, but you're surprised she's thinking of marrying him. In fact, you're not sure if you heard your sister correctly. What do you say to her?

   _____

3. Your friend tells you that he just got a large amount of money. You know that his car is falling apart. What do you say to him?

   _____

Teaching Point

Many times people want to express **sympathy** to someone else. At the same time, the person receiving the expression of sympathy must respond. We can look at such an interaction, structurally, as follow:

Person A expresses sympathy.	I'm really sorry about… *or* I was sorry to hear about…
Person B accepts the sympathy, expresses resignation and closes the interaction.	Yes, well, that's the way it goes. *or* What can you do? That's life. *or* Thank you. We're doing the best we can.

Language Note: "That's life" is not appropriate when accepting sympathy for the death of a friend or relative.

Activity 5 (Clip 4B)

Directions to the teacher:

Show the last part of the scene, with the sound on, from the point where Harry says, "How are you?" to the point where Harry says, "What happened with you guys?" Have students work in pairs A and B. Student A will write down Harry's expression of sympathy and his response to sympathy. Student B will write down Sally's expression of sympathy and her response to sympathy.

Directions to the students:

Divide into pairs. View the part of the scene that your teacher will play for you. Student A in the pair should write down Harry's expression of sympathy and his response to sympathy. Student B should write down Sally's expression of sympathy and her response to sympathy.

Harry's expression of sympathy (student A)

_____

Sally's response to sympathy (student B)

_____

Sally's expression of sympathy (student B)

_____

Harry's response to sympathy (student A)

_____

How are their responses to sympathy different?

_____

Scene 5 Harry & Sally in the Park

Activity 1

Directions to the teacher:

Pair the students. Have students look up the activity words listed below in an English-English dictionary. Have each pair write a dialogue in which the activity is performed. In other words, the students should perform apologies, compliments, and insults. The insults should use the words character flaw, hard as nails, and uptight.

Directions to the students:

In pairs, look up the three words in your English-English dictionary. Then, write dialogues for the activities. Perform your dialogues in front of the class.

Activities

apology

compliment

insult (Use these words: *character flaw, hard as nails, uptight*)

Directions to the students:

Now look up the words in the following list, and talk about them with your teacher. Write a short dialogue that uses both of the phrases. Perform your dialogue in front of the class.

to get in under the wire

statute of limitation

Activity 2 (Clip 5A)

Directions to the teacher:

Place the students in pairs. Have students try to fit the vocabulary from Activity 1 into the blanks in the dialogue that follows. After they have finished, play the first part of the scene, with the sound on, from the point where Harry says, "You know the first time we met, I really didn't like you that much" to the point where Harry says, "Ooh. I can just get in under the wire." Check for comprehension in a large group discussion.

Directions to the students:

Work with a partner to try to fit the vocabulary you practiced in Activity 1 into the following dialogue. When you have finished, your teacher will play this part of the scene for you. Check your work against the video.

Harry: You know, the first time we met, I really didn't like you that much–

Sally: I didn't like you.

Harry: Yeah, you did. You were just so _____ then. You're much softer now.

Sally: You know, I hate that kind of remark. It sounds like a
         _____, but really it's an _____.

Harry: Okay, you're still as _____.

Sally: I just didn't want to sleep with you, so you had to write it off as a
         _____ instead of dealing with the possibility that it might
         have something to do with you.

Harry: What's the _____ on apologies?

Sally: Ten years.

Harry: Ooh. I can just get in _____.

Teaching point

   In English, as in many other languages, we often use **contrasting pairs
of words** to emphasize meaning. This means that native speakers have a large
inventory of pairs of contrasting items, which can be used in a variety of
situations.

   Using contrasting pairs to clarify:

> **Examples: He's not *modest*. He's just *shy*.**
> **She's not *tired*. She's just *lazy*.**

   Using contrasting pairs to disagree:

> **Examples: I don't think that film was *interesting*. In**
> **fact, it was really *boring*.**
> **That test wasn't *challenging* at all. It was**
> **dead *easy*.**

Activity 3

Directions to the teacher:

   *Have students draw lines between the contrasting pairs of words in the matching
   columns that follow. Then, have them get into pairs and construct two dialogues using
   two different pairs of contrasting words.*

Directions to the students:

   Using your English-English dictionary, look up the meanings of any of the
   following words that you don't know. Then, draw lines between the words
   with contrasting meanings.

order	criticism
compliment	insult
suggestion	request

Now look at the lines from the film which use this contrastive structure.

Harry: Yeah, you did. You were just so uptight then. You're much softer now.

Sally: You know, I hate that kind of remark. It sounds like a *compliment*, but really it's an *insult*.

Work with a partner to fill in the blanks in speaker B's dialogue below with one of the contrasting pairs you identified earlier. Then write a sentence for speaker A that would lead to speaker B's response.

1. A: _____

_____

B: I hate that kind of remark. It sounds like a _____, but really it's a(n) _____.

After you have finished your dialogue, practice it with your partner.

Now work with your partner to fill in the blanks in speaker B's dialogue with another of the contrasting pairs you identified. Then, write a sentence for speaker A that would lead to speaker B's response.

2. A: _____

_____

B: I hate that kind of remark. It sounds like a _____, but really it's a(n) _____.

After you have finished your dialogue, practice it with your partner.

Activity 4 (Clip 5B)

Directions to the teacher:

Have students watch the second part of the scene, with the sound off, from the point where Harry and Sally stop walking, turn to each other, and Sally says, "Would you like to have dinner with me some time?" to the end of the scene. Then, ask them to answer the questions that follow.

Directions to the students:

View the part of the scene that your teacher will show you and answer the following questions.

1. Do you see any visual similarities between this scene and any scene from *Casablanca?*

2. Is there any similarity between the topic of conversation in this scene and the scene in *Casablanca?*

Activity 5 (Clip 5B)

Directions to the teacher:

Place the students in small groups. Have students watch the second part of the scene, with the sound on, from the point where Sally says, "Would you like to have dinner with me some time?" to the point where Sally says, "That's wonderful, Harry." Then, have them answer the following questions. Check for comprehension in a large group discussion.

Directions to the students:

In small groups, view the part of the scene that your teacher will show you. Then, answer the following questions. Share your answers with the members of your group.

1. What does Harry mean by "becoming friends"?
2. What do the words *woman friend* mean to Harry?
3. What's unusual about having a woman friend for Harry?

Scene 6 Harry & Sally on the Phone—watching *Casablanca*

Idioms in this scene:

to come down with something

on the side

to go around

Activity 1

Directions to the teacher:

Have students look up the following words in their English-English dictionaries.

Directions to the students:

Look up the definitions of the following words in your dictionaries. Write the meaning of each word in the blank next to that word.

depression _____

maintenance _____

miss _____

moan _____

Now, work with a partner to write a two-line dialogue that contains at least two of the words you just looked up. Discuss the answer to the question that follows.

A: _____

_____

B: _____

_____

1. What are some symptoms of depression?

Activity 2

Directions to the teacher:

Play the entire scene with the sound on and have the students work in small groups to answer the following questions.

Directions to the students:

Watch the scene your teacher plays for you. Then, work with a small group to answer the following questions.

1. How do Harry and Sally feel?

2. Why are they talking to each other late at night?

3. What are some examples of unusual behavior that Harry and Sally describe to each other? What do these unusual behaviors mean?

Behavior	Who	Meaning
1. _____	_____	_____
_____	_____	_____
2. _____	_____	_____
_____	_____	_____
3. _____	_____	_____
_____	_____	_____
4. _____	_____	_____
_____	_____	_____

Activity 3 (Clip 6A)

Directions to the teacher:

Play two times the part of the scene from where Harry says, "Now, you're telling me you would be happier with…" until the point where Harry says, "All right, fine. Have it your way." Have students fill in the blanks in the dialogue.

Directions to the students:

Watch the segment of the video and fill in the blanks in the following dialogue.

Harry: Now, you're telling me you would be happier with Victor Laslo than with Humphrey Bogart?

Sally: _____ did I say that?

Harry: When we _____ to New York.

Sally: I _____ said that. I _____ have said that.

Harry: All right, _____. Have it your _____.

Now answer the following questions:

1. Who is Victor Laslo?
2. Who is Humphrey Bogart?
3. What is the choice between them? Who made that choice?
4. What do Harry and Sally disagree about in this conversation?
5. Does Sally admit that Harry is right?
6. Does Harry admit Sally is right?

Teaching Point

Sometimes we define things by saying exactly what they are.

Example: A bicycle is a muscle-powered, two-wheel vehicle.

Other times we don't want to, or can't, give such a definition, so we use examples to define things.

Example: He's the kind of person you would trust with your deepest secret.
(e.g., He's trustworthy.)

Example: "You always say, 'Don't do this. Don't do that. Don't say this. Don't say that.' That's the kind of person you are."
(e.g., You are domineering.)

Activity 4 (Clip 6B)

Directions to the teacher:

> *Place the students in small groups. Play the part of the scene from the point where Harry says, "Ingrid Bergman. Now she's low maintenance" to the point where Harry says, "I know. High maintenance." Then have the students answer the questions.*

Directions to the students:

In small groups, watch the segment of the video that your teacher will play for your. Then, answer the following questions.

1. Who does Harry think is high maintenance, and who does Harry think is low maintenance?

2. What does L.M. mean in this conversation?

3. What example does Harry give of "high maintenance" behavior? To whom does it refer ? How do you know?

4. Are you a "high maintenance" or a "low maintenance" person? Give an example of how you are either a "high maintenance" or a "low maintenance" person.

Activity 5

Directions to the teacher:

> *Now play the whole scene again and have the students work together to answer the questions.*

Directions to the students:

Watch the whole scene again and answer these questions:

1. How would you characterize Sally and Harry's relationship at the end of this scene?

2. How does Sally feel about Harry?

3. How does Harry feel about Sally?

4. With whom do you have a relationship that is like the one between Sally and Harry in this scene?

Pre-Viewing Questions

1. A number of films, notably *Casablanca*, are referred to throughout *When Harry Met Sally*. What is the connection between these films and the story of Sally and Harry's relationship?

2. In the activities, you have seen Harry and Sally's relationship change over time. Do you think it will continue to change, or will it stay the same?

3. In this movie, Sally and Harry go through many changes as individuals. What are some of the important changes that they each experience? What causes the changes?

Post-Viewing Questions

1. Why do you think Harry and Sally keep making constant reference to old movies, and particularly to *Casablanca*?

2. Write down the various stages of Harry and Sally's relationship. You may wish to refer to the last scene of the movie, where Harry and Sally are "interviewed."

3. Explain some of the important events that change Sally. Explain some of the important events that change Harry. How are those events similar? How are they different?

Post-Viewing Activities

1. Pick one scene from the film, write out the dialogue, assign actors, and perform the scene in class.

2. Have a class debate on this statement:

   Men and women cannot be friends without eventually having a sexual relationship.

If You Liked This Film

You may wish to see these films about relationships between men and women:

The African Queen (1951) starring Katherine Hepburn and Humphrey Bogart. Directed by John Huston. (105 min. color).

It Happened One Night (1934) starring Claudette Colbert and Clark Gable. Directed by Frank Capra (105 min. black and white)

Appendix

Scripts for the Films

Gone with the Wind

Scene 1   In the Library at Twelve Oaks

Scene Description: The scene starts outside the library and continues in the library at Twelve
                   Oaks.

There are three voices: Scarlett, Ashley, and Rhett.

Scarlett: Ashley! Ashley!

Ashley: Scarlett! Who're you hiding from in here?

Scarlett: Uh.

Ashley: What are you up to?

Scarlett: Uh.

Ashley: Well, why aren't you upstairs resting with the other girls? What is this Scarlett, a secret?

Scarlett: Oh Ashley, Ashley, I love you.

Ashley: Scarlett.

Scarlett: I love you, I do.

Ashley: Well, isn't it enough that you've gathered every other man's heart today? You've
          always had mine. You cut your teeth on it.

Scarlett: Don't tease me now. Have I your heart my darling? I love you. I love you.

Ashley: You mustn't say such things. You'll hate me for hearing them.

Scarlett: Oh, I could never hate you. And I know you must care about me. Oh you do care,
          don't you?

Ashley: Yes, I care. Oh can't we go away and forget we ever said these things?

Scarlett: But how can we do that? Don't you, don't you want to marry me?

Ashley: I'm going to marry Melanie.

Scarlett: But you can't! Not if you care for me.

Ashley: Oh my dear, why must you make me say things that will hurt you? How can I make you
          understand? You're so young and unthinking. You don't know what marriage means.

Scarlett: I know I love you and I want to be your wife. You don't love Melanie.

Ashley: She's like me, Scarlett. She's part of my blood. We understand each other.

Scarlett: But you love me!

Ashley: How could I help loving you? You who have all the passion for life that I lack. But
          that kind of love isn't enough to make a successful marriage for two people who are
          as different as we are.

Scarlett: Why don't you say it, you coward? You're afraid to marry me. You'd rather live with
          that silly little fool who can't do anything except open her mouth to say "yes" "no"
          and raise a passel of mealy-mouthed brats just like her.

Ashley: You mustn't say things like that about Melanie.

Scarlett: Who are you to tell me I mustn't? You led me on! You made me believe you wanted to
          marry me.

Ashley: Now Scarlett, be fair. I never at any time…

Scarlett: You did! It's true you did! I'll hate you until I die. I can't think of anything bad enough
          to call you!

Rhett: Whew! Has the war started?

Scarlett:	Sir, you should have made your presence known!
Rhett:	In the middle of that beautiful love scene? That wouldn't have been very tactful, would it? But don't worry, your secret is safe with me.
Scarlett:	Sir, you are no gentleman!
Rhett:	And you miss are no lady. Don't think that I hold that against you! Ladies have never held any charm for me.
Scarlett:	First you take a low common advantage of me—then you insult me!
Rhett:	I meant it as a compliment. And I hope to see more of you when you're free of the spell of the elegant Mr. Wilkes. He doesn't strike me as half good enough for a girl of your—what was it?—"your passion for living"?
Scarlett:	How dare you! You aren't fit to wipe his boots!
Rhett:	And you were going to hate him for the rest of your life!

Scene 2 At the Confederate Ball

Scene Description: At the Confederate Ball. Scarlett is tapping her foot wistfully, looking at the dancing couples.

There are five voices: Dr. Meade; Scarlett; Melanie; Rhett; and a Confederate soldier.

Dr. Meade:	Ladies and gentlemen, I have important news, glorious news, another triumph for our magnificent men in arms. General Lee has completely whipped the enemy and swept the Yankee army northward from Virginia…
	And now a happy surprise for all of us. We have with us tonight that most daring of all blockade runners, whose fleet schooners slipping past the Yankee guns have brought us here the very woolens and laces we wear tonight. I refer, ladies and gentlemen, to that will-o'-the-wisp of the bounding main—none other than our friend from Charleston—Captain Rhett Butler!
Rhett:	Permit me.
Melanie:	Captain Butler, such a pleasure to see you again! I met you last at my husband's home.
Rhett:	That's kind of you to remember, Mrs. Wilkes.
Melanie:	Did you meet Captain Butler at Twelve Oaks, Scarlett?
Scarlett:	Yes, I…I think so!
Rhett:	Only for a moment, Mrs. Hamilton! It was in the library! You had broken something.
Scarlett:	Yes Captain Butler! I remember you!
Confederate Soldier:	The Confederacy asks for your jewelry on behalf of our noble cause.
Scarlett:	We aren't wearing any. We're in mourning.
Rhett:	Wait, on behalf of Mrs. Wilkes and Mrs. Hamilton.
Confederate Soldier:	Thank you Captain Butler.
Melanie:	Just a moment please!
Confederate Soldier:	But it's your wedding ring ma'am!
Melanie:	It may help my husband more off my finger!
Confederate Soldier:	Thank you.

Rhett: That was a very beautiful thing to do, Mrs. Wilkes.

Scarlett: Here, you can have mine too—for the cause.

Rhett: And you, Mrs. Hamilton. I know just how much that means to you!

Scene 3 In the Parlor at Aunt Pittypat's

Scene Description: The scene starts with Scarlett unwrapping a gift in the parlor of Aunt
                    Pittypat's. It ends with Rhett leaving.

There are two voices: Scarlett and Rhett.

(Clip 3A)

Scarlett: Oh, oh, oh, what a darling thing! Oh, Rhett, it's lovely, lovely. You didn't really
           bring it all the way from Paris just for me!

Rhett: Yes, I thought it was about time I got you out of that fake mourning. Next trip I'll
           bring you some green silk for a frock to match it!

Scarlett: Oh, Rhett.

Rhett: It's my duty to our brave boys at the front to keep our girls at home looking pretty.

Scarlett: It's so long since I've had anything new. How do I look?

Rhett: Awful. Just awful.

Scarlett: Why? What's the matter?

Rhett: This war's stopped being a joke when a girl like you doesn't know how to wear the
           latest fashion.

Scarlett: Oh, Rhett, let me do it. But Rhett, I don't know how I dare wear it!

Rhett: You will though, and another thing those pantalettes—I don't know a woman in
           Paris who wears pantalettes any more.

Scarlett: What do they…? You shouldn't talk about such things!

Rhett: You little hypocrite! You don't mind my knowing about them! Just my talking about
           them!

Scarlett: But Rhett, I really can't go on accepting these gifts, though you are awfully kind.

Rhett: I'm not kind. I'm just tempting you. I never give anything without expecting some-
           thing in return. I always get paid.

(Clip 3B)

Scarlett: If you think I'll marry you just to pay for the bonnet, I won't.

Rhett: Don't flatter yourself. I'm not a marrying man.

Scarlett: Well, I won't kiss you for it either.

Rhett: Open your eyes and look at me. No, I don't think I will kiss you, although you
           need kissing badly. That's what's wrong with you. You should be kissed and often
           and by someone who knows how.

Scarlett: I suppose you think you're the proper person.

Rhett: I might be if the right moment ever came.

Scarlett: You're a conceited black-hearted varmint, Rhett Butler, and I don't know why I let
           you come and see me.

Rhett: I'll tell you why Scarlett, because I'm the only man over 16 and under 60 who's
           around to show you a good time. But cheer up, the war can't last much longer.

(Clip 3C)

Scarlett: Really, Rhett, why?

Rhett: There's a little battle going on right now that ought to pretty well fix things one way or the other.

Scarlett: Oh Rhett—Is Ashley in it?

Rhett: So you still haven't got the wooden-headed Mr. Wilkes out of your mind! Yes, I suppose he's in it.

Scarlett: Oh, but tell me Rhett, where is it?

Rhett: Some little town in Pennsylvania, called Gettysburg!

Scene 4 In Rhett's Buggy in the Streets of Atlanta

Scene Description: The scene starts with Scarlett on the street as Atlanta is being evacuated. It continues in Rhett's buggy and ends with Scarlett getting out at Aunt Pittypat's.

There are two voices: Scarlett and Rhett.

(Clip 4A)

Rhett: Scarlett! Scarlett! Whoa! Whoa! Climb into this buggy. This is no day for walking. You'll get run over.

Scarlett: Oh Rhett, Rhett, drive me to Aunt Pitty's please.

Rhett: Panic's a pretty sight, isn't it? Whoa. That's just another of General Sherman's calling cards. He'll be paying us a visit soon.

Scarlett: I gotta get out of here. I gotta get out of here before the Yankees come.

Rhett: Leave your work at the hospital? Or have you had enough of death and lice and men chopped up? Well I suppose you weren't meant for sick men, Scarlett.

Scarlett: Don't talk to me like that, Rhett. I'm so scared. I wish I could get out of here.

(End of Clip 4A)

Rhett: Let's get out of here together. No use staying and letting the South come down around your ears. Too many nice places to go and visit—Mexico, London, Paris.

Scarlett: With you?

Rhett: Yes ma'am. A man who understands you and admires you for just what you are. I figure we belong together being the same sort. I'm waiting for you to grow up and get that sand-eyed Mr. Wilkes out of your heart. Well, I hear Mrs. Wilkes is going to have a baby in another month or so. Pretty hard loving a man with a wife and baby clinging to him.

Well, here we are. Are you going with me, or are you getting out?

Scarlett: I hate and despise you Rhett Butler, and I'll hate and despise you till I die.

Rhett: Oh no you won't Scarlett, not that long.

Scene 5 In Aunt Pitty's House and the Flight from Atlanta

Scene Description: The scene starts in Melanie's bedroom in Aunt Pitty's house and continues in the buggy, during the flight from Atlanta.

There are five voices: Scarlett; Rhett; Melanie; Prissy; and Voices in the Crowd.

Scarlett: Melly! Melly!

Rhett: Mrs. Wilkes, we're taking you to Tara.

Melanie: Tara.

Scarlett: It's the only way, Melly.

Melanie: No.

Scarlett: Sherman will burn the house over our heads if we stay. It's all right, Melly. It's all right.

Melanie: My baby. My poor baby.

Rhett: Have you the strength to put your arms around my neck?

Melanie: I think so. Ashley! Charles!

Rhett: What is it? What does she want?

Scarlett: Ashley's picture, Charles' sword. She wants us to bring them.

Rhett: Get them.

Scarlett: What-what's that?

Rhett: Our gallant lads must have set fire to the warehouses near the depot. Enough ammunition in the boxcars down there to blow us to Tara. We'll have to hurry if we're going to cross the tracks.

Scarlett: We're not going that way.

Rhett: We have to. The Donner Road's the only one the Yankees haven't cut yet.

Scarlett: Oh wait! I forgot to lock the front door. What are you laughing at?

Rhett: At you, locking the Yankees out.

Scarlett: Oh dear, I wish they'd hurry.

Rhett: I wouldn't be in such a hurry to see them go if I were you, my dear. With them goes the last semblance of law and order. Scavengers aren't wasting any time. Better get out of here fast.

Voices: There's a horse! Get it! Get that horse.

Prissy: Miss Scarlett!

Rhett: Haven't left much for the Yankees to take, have they? We'll have to make a dash for it before the fire reaches that ammunition. C'mon. Throw me your shawl. Sorry, you'll like it better if you don't see anything.

Scene 6 Return to Tara

Scene Description: The scene starts with Scarlett in front of Tara trying to find the house. It progresses to inside the house, and ends with her hugging her father in his study.

There are five voices: Scarlett, Prissy, Pa, Mammy, and Pork.

(Clip 6A)

Scarlett: Melly? Melly, we're home! We're at Tara! Hurry, move brute.

Prissy: Miss Scarlett, he's dead.

Scarlett: I can't see the house. Is it there? I can't see the house. Have they burned it? It's all right! It's all right! They haven't burned it! It's still there!

(Clip 6B)

Scarlett: Mother! Mother! I'm home! Mother, mother, I'm home. Mother, let me in. It's me, Scarlett! Oh, oh Pa, I'm home. I'm home.

Pa: Katie, Katie Scarlett, oh darling.

Scarlett: Mammy, mammy, I'm home.

Mammy: Scarlett, oh Scarlett, honey child.

Scarlett: Oh Mammy, I'm so, so...where's Mother?

Mammy: Why, Miss Sue Ellen and Miss Corrine they was sick with the typhoid. They had it bad. But they's doing all right now. Just weak like little kittens.

Scarlett: But, but where's mother.

Mammy: Well, Miss Ellen she went down to nurse that Emmie Slattery, that white trash, and she took down with it too and last night she...

Scarlett: Mother, mother, mother, mother?

Mammy: Miss Scarlett, honey.

Pork: If there's anything I can do, Miss Scarlett.

(Clip 6C)

Scarlett: What'd you do with Miss Melly?

Mammy: Don't you worry your pretty head about Miss Melly, child. I done slapped her in bed already along with the baby.

Scarlett: You better put that cow I brought into the barn Pork.

Pork: There ain't no barn no more, Miss Scarlett. The Yankees done burned it for fire-wood.

Mammy: They used the house for their headquarters, Miss Scarlett.

Pork: They camped all around the place.

Scarlett: Yankees in Tara!

Mammy: Yes'm, yes and they stole most everything they didn't burn, all the clothes, and all the rugs and even Miss Ellen's rosaries.

Scarlett: I'm starving, Pork. Get me something to eat.

Mammy: There ain't nothing to eat, honey. They took it all.

Scarlett: All the chickens? Everything?

Pork: They took them the first day, and what'd they leave they carried off across their saddles.

(Clip 6D)

Scarlett: Don't tell me anymore about what they did. What's this Pa? Whiskey?

Pa: Yes, daughter. Katie Scarlett, that's enough. You're not knowing spirits. You'll make yourself tipsy.

Scarlett: I hope it makes me drunk. I'd like to be drunk. Oh Pa, what are those papers?

Pa: Bonds. They're all we've saved. All we have left. Bonds.

Scarlett: But what kind of bonds, Pa?

Pa: Why Confederate bonds, of course, daughter.

Scarlett: Confederate bonds! What good are they to anybody?

Pa: I'll not have you talking like that, Katie Scarlett.

Scarlett: Oh Pa, what are we going to do with no money and nothing to eat?

Pa: We must ask your mother. That's it. We must ask Mrs. O'Hara.

Scarlett: Ask mother?

Pa: Yes, Mrs. O'Hara will know what's to be done. Now don't be bothering me. Go out for a ride. I'm busy.

Scarlett: Oh, Pa. Don't worry about anything. Katie Scarlett's home. You needn't worry.

Dances with Wolves

Scene 1 On the Battlefield

Scene Description: This scene starts at the very beginning of the movie, while the credits are still flashing. The scene begins when a rifle, with a cap on top, comes into view. The scene ends with Dunbar hugging his horse, getting ready for a second ride across the field.

There are five voices:. The voices are those of Dunbar, an enlisted man, an officer, a soldier, another enlisted man, and a Confederate soldier.

Officer:	Glass.
	Is that Tucker's men?
Soldier:	Yes, Sir, I think it is.
Officer:	How long has it been like this?
Soldier:	We just found them this morning, sir. They've been here for two days.
Enlisted Man:	That you lieutenant?
	(muttered word) son of a bitches.
	You'd better take cover.
	I ain't kidding.
	These boys are shooters.
	Go on.
	You went to hospital?
Dunbar:	It was no good.
	What's going on here?
Enlisted Man:	What's going on here? That seems to be the question all right.

See, you could ask the major, but he don't know. He's busy. He's busy trying to figure out how come the officer's mess run out of peach ice cream.

And of course, you've got the general. He come up to see the show. All he knows is there ain't no show.

Now the major he's looking at the general. He's thinking to himself, I'd better do something. You know what that means? I sure as hell don't want to be the first one across this field.

They're supposed to be beat up just like us. Hell, everybody knows Tucker's men are tough as Cobbs'. So far the only thing been killed out here is three milking cows.

Course that's about to change.

Know something the boys are saying? If we ain't gonna fight, we could just settle this whole business with a little high stakes poker. Wouldn't that be exciting?

Soldier:	What is it, sir?
Officer:	Looks like a suicide.

Confederate Soldier: Tucker!

Second Enlisted Man: What'd you say to him?

Enlisted Man: I didn't say nothing.

(Sounds of assorted rabble.)

Scene 2 In the Office

Scene Description: Dunbar is inside the office of the crazy officer talking to him. The scene ends with Dunbar leaving the office.

There are two voices: Dunbar and the crazy officer.

Crazy Officer: Lieutenant John J. Dunbar

Lieutenant John J. Dunbar?

Dunbar: Yes, sir.

Crazy Officer: Yes, sir. Indian fighter, huh?

Dunbar: Excuse me.

Crazy Officer: Well it says here that you're to be posted on the frontier. The frontier is Indian country. I quickly deduce that you're an Indian fighter. I did not ascend to this position by being stupid.

Dunbar: No sir.

Crazy Officer: It says here that you've been decorated.

Dunbar: Yes, sir.

Crazy Officer: And they sent you here to be posted?

Dunbar: Actually, sir, I'm here at my own request.

Crazy Officer: Really, why?

Dunbar: I've always wanted to see the frontier.

Crazy Officer: You want to see the frontier?

Dunbar: Yes sir, before it's gone.

Crazy Officer: Such a smart lad coming straight to me. Sir Knight, I am sending you on a knight's errand. You will report to Captain Hargill at the further-most outpost of the realm—Fort Sedgewick. My personal seal will assure your safety through many miles of wild and hostile country.

Dunbar: I was wondering…

Crazy Officer: Yes?

Dunbar: I was wondering—how will I be getting there?

Crazy Officer: You think I don't know?

Dunbar: No, sir.

Crazy Officer: You think I don't know.

Dunbar: No, sir. It's just that I don't know.

Crazy Officer: Hold your tongue. I happen to be in a generous mood and I will grant your boon. See that peasant out there? He calls himself Timmons. He's going to your Fort Sedgewick this very afternoon. You can ride with him if you like. He knows the way. Thank you. That is all.

Sir knight! I have just pissed in my pants and nobody can do anything about it.

Scene 3 With the Wolf

Scene Description: Dunbar is trying to get the wolf to eat a piece of bacon. The scene ends
with Dunbar on the prairie, reading his journal.

There are two voices: Dunbar and Kicking Bird.

Dunbar: Uhm. Uhm.
C'mon Two Socks. Bacon.
Two Socks, like Cisco has become a trusted friend. He still won't eat from my
hand but his keen eyes and ears never fail to alert me when something is
wrong.

Kicking Bird: Tatanka?

Dunbar: No, I haven't seen any buffalo.
I'm sorry.

Are you hungry?

Are you hungry?

I have food.

I have a—I have a lot of food.

Kicking Bird: (Speaks Lakota —no subtitles. Obviously, these are words of comprehension
and negation.)

Dunbar: Nothing I have been told about these people is correct. They are not beggars
and thieves. They are not the bogey men they have been made out to be. On
the contrary, they are polite guests and have a familiar humor I enjoy.

Real communication is slow however and the quiet one is as frustrated as I
am. Most of our progress has been built on the basis of failure rather than success. I've thought to inquire about the woman I found on the prairie, whether
she lived or   not, but it seems far too complicated a subject given our limitations. One thing is clear, however, there are no buffalo, and it weighs heavy
on their minds. Yesterday's meeting was the best yet. It seems I've been invited
to the village. I am looking forward to going.

Scene 4 In the Tent

Scene Description: Dunbar is in a tent, whittling a piece of wood. Two native Americans enter,
talk, and leave.

There are three voices: Dunbar, Kicking Bird, and Stands with a Fist.

Dunbar: A war party is going against the Pawnee soon, and I have asked to go. I sense
that I made a mistake in doing so but I could not bring myself to take it back.
They are my friends and from what little I gather the Pawnee have been very
hard on these people. I hope I have not overstepped my bounds.

Come in please.

Sit down.

Kicking Bird: (Lakota words). [Not subtitled.]

Stand with a Fist:
Kicking Bird wants to know why you want to make war on the Pawnee. They
have done nothing to you.

Dunbar: They are Sioux enemies.

Stands with a Fist:
>   (Lakota words). [Not subtitled.]

Kicking Bird: (Lakota words). [Not subtitled.]

Stands with a Fist:
>   Only, only Sioux warriors to go.

Dunbar: Well then tell him that I have been a warrior longer than many of the young men who will go on this war party. Tell him.

Stands with a Fist:
>   (Lakota words). [Not subtitled.]

Kicking Bird: (Lakota words). [Not subtitled.]

Stands with a Fist:
>   He said that the Sioux way of being a warrior is not the white way. You are not ready.

Dunbar: I know. I understand, but tell him…tell him that I cannot learn these ways in camp.

Kicking Bird: (Lakota words). [Not subtitled.]

Stands with a Fist:
>   He also asks that you watch over his family while he is gone. This thing he asks is a great honor for you.

Dunbar: Tell him that I would be happy to watch over his family.

Stands with a Fist:
>   (Lakota words). [Not subtitled.]

Kicking Bird: (Lakota words). [Not subtitled.]

Stands with a Fist:
>   He thanks Dances with Wolves for coming.

Dunbar: Who is Dances with Wolves?

Stands with a Fist:
>   It is the name which all the people are calling you now.

Dunbar: Dances with…That's right. That day. Dances with Wolves. How do you say it?

Stands with a Fist:
>   (Lakota words). [Not subtitled.]

Dunbar: (Lakota words). [Not subtitled.]

Kicking Bird: (Lakota words). [Not subtitled.]

Stands with a Fist:
>   (Lakota words). [Not subtitled.]

Dunbar: (Lakota words). [Not subtitled.]

Scene 5 At the River

Scene Description: Dances with Wolves and Stands with a Fist are sitting on a log near a river. She is getting water from the river. The scene ends when she runs off.

There are two voices: Dances with Wolves and Stands with a Fist.

Dances with Wolves: How did you get your name?

Stands with a Fist: I was not very old when I came to be with the people and I was made to work. I worked every day very hard. There was a one…one woman who didn't like me much and she used to call me bad names and sometimes she—amapre—beat? me.

Um. One day she was calling me these bad names with her face in my face and I hit her. I was not very big but she fell down. She fell hard and didn't move and then I stood over her with my fist and asked if there was any other woman who wanted to call me bad names. No one bothered me after that day.

Dances with Wolves: No, I, I wouldn't think so. Show me. Show me where you hit her.

Why are you not married?

I'm sorry. I'm sorry.

Stands with a Fist: I have to go.

Dances with Wolves: I'm sorry. Can I help you?

Scene 6 At the Fort

Scene Description: In this scene, Dances with Wolves is back at the fort. He has been clubbed and is in the process of waking up. The scene ends with the leering face of the sergeant standing over Dances with Wolves.

There are six voices in the scene: Spotty, Sergeant, Dances with Wolves, Officer 1, Officer 2, and another voice.

Sergeant: Spotty?

Spotty!

Spotty: Yeah, Sergeant?

Sergeant: Tell the major he's waking up. Move your worthless ass.
You got yourself a hell of a shiner, didn't you?

Another Voice: The Major's coming through.

Officer 1: Well, does he speak English?

Sergeant: I don't know sir.

Speak English?

You talk English?

TALK!

Dances with Wolves: I speak English.

Officer 1: Who are you?

Dances with Wolves: Lieutenant John J. Dunbar. This is my post.

Officer 1: Why are you dressed like this?

Dances with Wolves:	I came out from Fort Hays last April but there was nobody here.
Officer 2:	Do you have proof of that?
Dances with Wolves:	My journal's on the bunk in my quarters. My orders are in the journal. It'll…it'll tell you everything.
Officer 2:	Spotty, you and Edwards were the first ones here. Did you find anything? A journal?
Spotty:	Nah, we didn't find nothing, sir.
Officer 2:	Where's Edwards?
Spotty:	He's outside.
	Hey, he didn't find nothing either.
Officer 2:	Somebody find me Edwards.
Sergeant:	Turned Injun, didn't you, didn't you?

To Kill a Mockingbird

Scene 1 Jem & Dill Talk about Boo

Scene Description: A conversation between Jem and Dill about Boo Radley. Jem, Scout, and Dill are present. This scene occurs shortly after Jem and Scout have met Dill. The kids are near a tree, looking at the Radley house.

There are two voices: Jem and Dill.

Jem:	There goes the meanest man that ever took a breath of life.
Dill:	Why is he the meanest man?
Jem:	Well for one thing he has a boy named Boo that he keeps chained to a bed in the house over yonder. C'mon. See? He lives over there. Boo only comes out at night when you're asleep and it's pitch dark. When you wake up at night you can hear him. Once I heard him scratching on our screen door but he was gone by the time Atticus got there.
Dill:	Wonder what he does in there? Wonder what he looks like?
Jem:	Well, judging from his tracks he's about six and a half feet tall. He eats raw squirrels and all the cats he can catch. There's a long jagged scar that runs all the way across his face. His teeth are yellow and rotten. His eyes are popped and he drools most of the time.

Scene 2 Atticus & Ewell outside the Courtroom

Scene Description: A conversation between Atticus and Ewell about Tom Robinson and the rape case. This scene takes place in the courthouse after Atticus has told the kids to go home.

Mr. Ewell:	Cap'n, I'm real sorry that they picked you to defend that nigger that raped my Mayella. I don't know why I didn't kill him myself instead of going to the sheriff. I would have saved you and the sheriff and the taxpayers lots of trouble.
Mr. Finch:	Excuse me, Mr. Ewell. I'm very busy.
Mr. Ewell:	Hey Cap'n. Somebody told me just now that they thought that you believed Tom Robinson's story against our'n. You know what I said? I said, "you wrong man. You dead wrong. Mr. Finch ain't taking his story against our'n." Well they was wrong, wasn't they?
Mr. Finch:	I've been appointed to defend Tom Robinson. Now that he's been charged that's what I intend to do.
Mr. Ewell:	You taking his story?
Mr. Finch:	If you'll excuse me Mr. Ewell?
Mr. Ewell:	What kind of man are you? You got children of your own.

Scene 3 The Children near the Radley House

Scene Description: This scene takes place at night. The three principle characters are the children, Jem, Scout, and Dill. It begins with the children sneaking along the fence towards the Radley house. From there, Jem goes to the porch, where he encounters a shadow. The scene ends with the townspeople congregated on the Radleys' front lawn. Jem and Scout are on their front lawn, looking at the Radley house. There is no dialogue in this scene.

Scene 4 The Dining Room at the Finch Home

Scene Description: A lunch time conversation between Jem and Atticus in which the meaning of the title of the movie is made clear. Atticus, Jem, Scout, and Walter Cunningham are present. Lunch is being served.

There are two voices: Jem and Atticus.

Jem: How old were you when you got your first gun Atticus?

Atticus: Thirteen or 14. I remember when my daddy gave me that gun he told me that I should never point at anything in the house and that he'd rather I shoot at tin cans in the back yard. But he said that sooner or later he supposed the temptation to go after birds would be too much and that I could shoot all the blue jays I wanted if I could hit 'em but to remember it was a sin to kill a mockingbird.

Jem: Why?

Atticus: Well I reckon 'cause mockingbirds don't do anything but make music for us to enjoy. Don't eat people's gardens; don't nest in the corn cribs. They don't do one thing but just sing their hearts out for us.

Scene 5 The Mad Dog

Scene Description: This is the "mad dog" scene. The scene starts with the children running into the house to inform Calpurnia of the dog. In the course of the scene, Atticus arrives and shoots the dog. The scene ends as Atticus drives away and the children look surprised.

Scene 6 Atticus & Jem at the Robinsons'

Scene Description: A long visual sequence which starts in the car on the way to the Robinson's house and ends with Jem finding a spelling medal in the tree in front of the Radleys.

There are seven voices: Scout, Atticus, David, Helen, Jem, Mr. Ewell, and Cal.

Scout: Who's Helen Robinson?

Atticus: She's the wife of the man I'm defending.

Good evening David.

David: Evening.

Atticus: Good evening, Helen.

Helen: Evening, Mr. Finch.

Atticus: I came over to tell you about my visit with Tom.

Helen: Yes, sir.

Atticus: And to let you know I got a postponement of the trial to give things a chance to cool down.

Jem: Would you tell my daddy to come out here please?

Mr. Ewell: You nigger lover.

Atticus: No need to be afraid of him son. He's all bluff.

Mr. Ewell: Nigger lover!

Atticus: There's a...there's a lot of ugly things in this world son. I wish I could keep them all away from you. That's never possible.

Cal, you wait 'til I get Scout in bed. I'll drive you home.

Cal: Yes, sir.

Atticus: Jem, do you mind staying here with Scout 'til I get Cal home?

Jem: No, sir.

Cal: Good night, Jem.

Jem: Good night, Cal.

Atticus! Atticus! Atticus!

Casablanca

Scene 1 The Refugee Trail

Scene Description: A map of Europe and Africa with scenes of refugees fleeing.

Character: off-screen narrator

> With the coming of the Second World War, many eyes in imprisoned Europe turned hopefully, or desperately, toward the freedom of the Americas. Lisbon became the great embarkation point, but not everybody could get to Lisbon directly, and so a tortuous, roundabout refugee trail sprang up—Paris to Marseille—across the Mediterranean to Oran—then by train, or auto, or foot across the rim of Africa—to Casablanca in French Morocco. Here the fortunate ones—through money, or influence, or luck—might obtain exit visas and scurry to Lisbon, and from Lisbon to the New World. But the others wait in Casablanca, and wait, and wait, and wait.

Scene 2 Police Question Suspects

Scene Description: The scene starts with a man ripping a document from a teletype machine. It moves to scenes of people being arrested and ends with a man being shot under a sign which reads, "Liberte, Egalite, Fraternite."

There are four voices: Official in office, man stopped by police, first policeman, second policeman

Official: To all officers. Two German couriers carrying important official documents murdered on train from Oran. Murderer and possible accomplices headed for Casablanca. Round up all suspicious characters and search them for stolen documents. Important.

First Policeman:
  May we see your papers?

Man: I don't think I have them on me.

First Policeman:
  In that case we'll have to ask you to come along.

Man: Wait. It's possible that—yes. Here they are.

Second Policeman:
  These papers expired three weeks ago. You'll have to come along. Halt! Halt!

Scene 3 Rick & Ugarte at Rick's

Scene Description: The scene starts and ends in the cafe. It is a conversation between Rick and Ugarte.

There are three voices: Rick Blaine, Ugarte, Waiter.

(Clip 3A)

Ugarte: You know, Rick, watching you just now with the Deutsche Bank, one would think you've been doing this all your life.

Rick: Well, what makes you think I haven't?

Ugarte: Oh, nothing. But when you first came to Casablanca, I thought…

Rick: You thought what?

Ugarte: What right do I have to think? May I? Too bad about those two German couriers, wasn't it?

Rick: They got a lucky break. Yesterday they were just two German clerks; today they're the honored dead.

(Clip 3B)

Ugarte: You are a very cynical person, Rick, if you'll forgive me for saying so.

Rick: I'll forgive you.

Ugarte: Thank you. Will you have a drink with me please?

Rick: No.

Ugarte: Oh, I forgot you never drink with any... I'll have another, please.

Waiter: Yes, monsieur.

Ugarte: You despise me, don't you?

Rick: Well, if I gave you any thought I probably would.

(Clip 3C)

Ugarte: But why? Oh, you object to the kind of business I do, huh? But think of all those poor refugees who must rot in this place if I didn't help them. Well, that's not so bad. Through ways of my own, I provide them with exit visas.

Rick: For a price, Ugarte, for a price.

Ugarte: But think of all the poor devils who can't beat Renaud's price. Well, I get it for them for half. Is that so parasitic?

Rick: I don't mind a parasite. I object to a cut-rate one.

Ugarte: Well, Rick, after tonight I'll be through with the whole business, and I'm leaving, finally, this Casablanca.

Rick: Who's supplying your visa, Renaud or yourself?

Ugarte: Myself. I found myself much more reasonable.

(Clip 3D)

Ugarte: Look, Rick. You know what this is? Something that even you have never seen. Letters of transit signed by General De Gaulle. Cannot be rescinded, not even questioned.

One moment. Tonight I'll be selling those for more money than even I have ever dreamed of, and then "adio" Casablanca. You know, Rick, I have many a friend in Casablanca, but somehow, just because you despise me, you are the only one I trust. Will you keep these for me please?

Rick: For how long?

Ugarte: Oh, perhaps an hour, perhaps a little longer.

Rick: I don't want them here overnight.

Ugarte: Don't be afraid of that. Please keep them for me. Thank you. I knew I could trust you.

(Clip 3E)

Ugarte: ...Waiter! I'll be expecting some people. If anybody asks for me, I'll be right here.

Waiter: Yes, monsieur.

Ugarte: Rick, I hope you're more impressed with me now. If you'll forgive me, I'll share my good luck with your roulette wheel.

Rick: Just a moment. I heard a rumor those two German couriers were carrying letters of transit.

Ugarte: Huh? Oh, I've heard that rumor, too. Poor devils.

Rick: Yes, you're right, Ugarte. I am a little more impressed with you.

Scene 4 Rick & Louis in Rick's Office

Scene Description: In the private quarters of Rick's Cafe, near the safe. A conversation with
Louis about Victor Laslo. The scene ends with Louis going to meet Strasser.
There are two voices: Rick, Louis, and a Soldier

(Clip 4A)

Rick: Louis you got something on your mind. Why don't you spill it?

Louis: How observant you are. Matter of fact I wanted to give you a word of advice.

Rick: Yeah, brandy…

Louis: Thank you. Rick there are many exit visas sold in this cafe but we know that you've
never sold one. That is the reason we permit you to remain open.

Rick: I thought it was because I let you win at roulette.

Louis: That is another reason. There is a man arrived in Casablanca on his way to America.
He will offer a fortune to anyone who will furnish him with an exit visa.

Rick: What's his name?

Louis: Victor Laslo.

Rick: Victor Laslo!

Louis: Rick, that is the first time I have ever seen you so impressed.

Rick: Well, he's succeeded in impressing half the world.

Louis: It's my duty to see that he doesn't impress the other half. Rick, Laslo must never
reach America. He stays in Casablanca.

(Clip 4B)

Rick: It'll be interesting to see how he manages.

Louis: Manages what?

Rick: His escape.

Louis: Oh, but I just told you…

Rick: Stop it! He escaped from a concentration camp. The Nazis have been chasing him all
over Europe.

Louis: This is the end of the chase.

Rick: Twenty thousand francs says it isn't.

Louis: Is that a serious offer?

Rick: I just paid out 20. I'd like to get it back.

Louis: Make it 10. I'm only a poor corrupt official.

Rick: OK.

Louis: Done. No matter how clever he is he still needs an exit visa, or I should say two.

Rick: Why two?

Louis: He is traveling with a lady.

Rick: He'll take one.

Louis: I think not. I've seen the lady. And if he did not leave her in Marseille or in Oran, he
certainly won't leave her in Casablanca.

Rick: Well maybe he's not quite as romantic as you are.

Louis: It doesn't matter. There is no exit visa for him.

(Clip 4C)

Rick: Louis, whatever gave you the impression that I might be interested in helping Laslo escape?

Louis: Because, my dear Rick, I suspect that under that cynical shell you're at heart a sentimentalist. Oh laugh if you will but I happen to be familiar with your record. Let me point out just two items: in 1935, you ran guns to Ethiopia. In 1936, you fought in Spain on the Loyalist side.

Rick: And got well paid for it on both occasions.

Louis: The winning side would have paid you much better.

Rick: Maybe.

Louis: Uh huh.

Rick: Well it seems that you're determined to keep Laslo here.

Louis: I have my orders.

Rick: Oh, I see, Gestapo spank.

Louis: My dear Rick, you overestimate the influence of the Gestapo. I don't interfere with them and they don't interfere with me. In Casablanca, I am master of my fate.

Soldier: Major Strasser is here, sir.

Rick: You were saying…

Louis: Excuse me.

Scene 5 Laslo, Ilse & Louis at a Table in Rick's

Scene Description: At a table in Rick's Cafe. Louis comes up and introduces himself. Laslo, Louis, and Ilse talk about Rick.

There are four voices: Laslo, Louis, Ilse, and Emil

Louis: Mssr. Laslo is it not?

Laslo: Yes.

Louis: I am Captain Renaud. Prefect of Police.

Laslo: Yes, what is it you want?

Louis: Merely to welcome you to Casablanca and to wish you a pleasant stay. It isn't often we have so distinguished a visitor.

Laslo: Thank you. I hope you will forgive me Captain. The present French administration hasn't always been so cordial. May I present Miss Ilse Lund.

Louis: I was informed you were the most beautiful woman ever to visit Casablanca. That was a gross understatement.

Ilse: You are very kind.

Laslo: Won't you join us?

Louis: If you will permit me. Oh no, Emil please, a bottle of your best champaign and put it on my bill.

Emil: Very well sir.

Laslo: Captain Please…

Louis: Please Mssr. It is a little game we play. They put it on the bill. I tear up the bill. It is very convenient.

Ilse: Captain—the boy who is playing the piano. There is somewhere I've seen him.

Louis: Sam?

Ilse: Yes.

Louis: He came from Paris with Rick.

Ilse: Rick? Who's he?

Louis: Mademoiselle, you are in Rick's and Rick is…

Ilse: Is what?

Louis: Well Mademoiselle, he's the kind of man if I were a woman and I weren't around, I should be in love with Rick. But what a fool I am talking to a beautiful woman about another man. Oh, excuse me…

Scene 6 Rick & Ilse Meet Again

Scene Description: At a table in Rick's Cafe. Ilse, Rick, Laslo, and Louis are all talking and Rick is reminiscing about the last time he saw Ilse. The scene ends with Laslo and Ilse leaving.

Characters: Louis, Laslo, Rick, Ilse, and Emil

Louis: Well, you were asking about Rick and here he is. Mademoiselle may I present…

Ilse: Hello Rick.

Louis: Oh, you've already met Rick, Mademoiselle. Well then perhaps you also…

Ilse: This is Mr. Laslo.

Laslo: How do you do?

Rick: How do you do.

Laslo: One hears a great deal about Rick in Casablanca.

Rick: And about Victor Laslo everywhere.

Laslo: Won't you join us for a drink?

Louis: Oh no Rick…

Rick: Thanks, I will.

Louis: Well, a precedent is being broken. Oh Emil…

Laslo: This is a very interesting cafe. I congratulate you.

Rick: I congratulate you.

Laslo: What for?

Rick:

Laslo: Thank you. I try.

Rick: We all try. You succeed.

Louis: I can't get over you two. She was asking about you earlier Rick in a way that made me extremely jealous.

Ilse: I wasn't sure you were the same. Let's see the last time we met…

Rick: Was the Belle Aurora.

Ilse: How nice. You remembered. But of course that was the day the Germans marched into Paris.

Rick: Not an easy day to forget.

Ilse: No.

Rick: I remember every detail. The Germans wore grey. You wore blue.

Ilse: Yes. I put that dress away. When the Germans march out, I'll wear it again.

Louis: Rick, you're becoming quite human. I suppose we have you to thank for that Mademoiselle.

Laslo: Yes, I don't wish to be the one to say it, but it's late.

Louis: So it is. And we have a curfew here in Casablanca. It would never do for the chief of police to be found drinking after hours and have to fine himself.

Laslo: I hope we didn't overstay our welcome.

Rick: Not at all.

Else: Your check, sir.

Rick: Oh, it's my party.

Louis: Another precedent gone. This has been a very interesting evening. I'll call you a cab. Gasoline rationing. Time of night.

Laslo: We'll come again.

Rick: Any time.

Ilse: Say goodnight to Sam for me.

Rick: I will.

Ilse: There's still nobody in the world who can play "As Time Goes By" like Sam.

Rick: He hasn't played it in a long time.

When Harry Met Sally

Scene 1 Harry Meets Sally

Scene Description: Outside of the University of Chicago. Sally is in a car. Harry is saying goodbye to his girlfriend Amanda Reese.

There are three voices: Amanda, Harry, and Sally

Amanda: Oh, hi, Sally. Sally, this is Harry Burns. Harry, this is Sally Albright.

Harry: Nice to meet you.

Sally: You want to drive the first shift?

Harry: No, no, you're there already, you can start.

Sally: Back's open.

Amanda: Call me.

Harry: I'll call as soon as I get there.

Amanda: Call me from the road.

Harry: I'll call you before that.

Amanda: I love you.

Harry: I love you.

Sally: Sorry.

Harry: I miss you already.

Amanda: I miss you.

Harry: Bye.

Scene 2 On the way to New York

Scene Description: In the car on the way to New York. Harry and Sally are discussing
Casablanca. The scene starts as they round the hill going towards the
diner and ends inside the diner.

There are two voices: Harry and Sally

Sally: You're wrong.

Harry: I'm not wrong.

Sally: You're wrong.

Harry: He wants her to leave. That's why he puts her on the plane.

Sally: I don't think she wants to stay.

Harry: Of course she wants to stay. Wouldn't you rather be with Humphrey Bogart than
the other guy?

Sally: I don't want to spend the rest of my life in Casablanca married to a man who runs
a bar. That probably sounds very snobbish to you, but I don't.

Harry: You'd rather be in a passionless marriage—

Sally: —and be First Lady of Czechoslovakia—

Harry: —than live with the man…you've had the greatest sex of your life with, just
because he owns a bar and that is all he does.

Sally: Yes, and so would any woman in her right mind. Women are very practical.

Even Ingrid Bergman, which is why she gets on the plane at the end of the movie.

Harry: Oh, I understand.

Sally: What? What?

Harry: Nothing.

Sally: What?

Harry: Forget about it.

Sally: What? What? Forget about what?

Harry: It's not important.

Sally: Now just tell me.

Harry: Obviously you haven't had great sex yet.

Scene 3 Sally & Joe at the Airport

Scene Description: At the airport. Sally and Joe are kissing and saying goodbye as Harry
walks up.

There are three voices: Harry, Sally, and Joe

Harry: Joe—I thought it was you. I thought it was you. Harry Burns.

Joe: Harry, Harry, how ya doing?

Harry: Good. How you doing?

Joe: I'm just fine. I'm doing fine.

Harry: I was just walking by, and I thought it was you, and there it is, it's you.

Joe: Yeah, yeah, it was.

Harry: You still with the D.A.'s Office?

Joe: No, I switched to the other side.

Harry: Oh.

Joe: What about you?

Harry: I'm working with a small company. We do political consulting.

Joe: Oh yeah?

Harry: Yeah, it's been great. Yeah.

Joe: Oh Harry, this is Sally Albright. Harry Burns. Harry and I used to live in the same building.

Harry: Well, listen, I got a plane to catch. It was really good to see you, Joe.

Joe: You too Harry.

Harry:

Sally: Thank God he couldn't place me. I drove from college to New York with him five
        years ago and it was the longest night of my life.

Joe: What happened?

Sally: He made a pass at me, and when I said no—he was going with a girlfriend of mine—
        oh God, I can't remember her name. Don't get involved with me, Joe, I am twenty-six
        years old and I can't even remember the name of the girl I was such good friends
        with that I wouldn't get involved with her boyfriend.

Joe: So what happened?

Sally: When?

Joe: When he made a pass at you–you said no.

Sally: Uh …I said we could just be friends, and–this part I remember—he said that men and women could never really be friends. Do you think that's true?

Joe: No.

Sally: Do you have any women friends? Just friends?

Joe: No, but I will get one if it's important to you.

Sally: Amanda Reese. That was her name. Thank God.

Joe: I'm going to miss you. I love you.

Sally: You do?

Joe: Yes.

Sally: I love you.

Scene 4 In the Bookstore

Scene Description: In a bookstore in New York. Sally and her friend are talking when her friend notices Harry.

There are three voices: Harry, Sally, and Marie

(Clip 4A)

Marie: Someone is staring at you in Personal Growth.

Sally: I know him. You'd like him. He's married.

Marie: Who is he?

Sally: Harry Burns. He's a political consultant.

Marie: He's cute.

Sally: You think he's cute?

Marie: How do you know he's married?

Sally: Cause the last time I saw him, he was getting married.

Marie: When was that?

Sally: Six years ago.

Marie: So he might not be married anymore.

Sally: Also he's obnoxious.

(End of Clip 4A)

Marie: This is just like in the movies, remember in *The Lady Vanished*, when she says to him, "You are the most obnoxious man I have ever met"—

Sally: —"the most contemptible" —

Marie: And they fall madly in love.

Sally: Also, he never remembers me.

Harry: Sally Albright—

Sally: Hi, Harry—

Harry: I thought it was you.

Sally: It is. This is Marie …… was Marie.

(Clip 4B)

Harry: How are you?

Sally: Fine.

Harry: How's Joe?

Sally: Fine. I hear he's fine.

Harry: You're not with Joe anymore?

Sally: We just broke up.

Harry: Oh, I'm sorry. That's too bad.

Sally: Yeah, well, you know. Yeah. So, what about you?

Harry: I'm fine.

Sally: How's married life?

Harry: Not so good. I'm getting a divorce.

Sally: Oh, I'm sorry. I'm really sorry.

Harry: Yeah. Well. What are you going to do? What happened with you guys?

Scene 5 Harry & Sally in the Park

Scene Description: Harry and Sally are walking in a park and along a street in New York City.
Characters: Harry and Sally

Sally: At least I got the apartment.

Harry: That's what everybody says to me, too. But really, what's so hard about finding an apartment? What you do is, you read the obituary column. Yeah. You find out who died, go to the building, and then you tip the doorman. What they can do to make it easier is to combine the obituaries with the real estate section, see, and then you have, "Mr. Klein died today, leaving a wife, two children, and a spacious three-bedroom apartment with a wood-burning fireplace."

(Clip 5A)

Harry: You know, the first time we met, I really didn't like you that much—

Sally: I didn't like you.

Harry: Yeah, you did. You were just so uptight then. You're much softer now.

Sally: You know, I hate that kind of remark. It sounds like a compliment, but really it's an insult.

Harry: Okay, you're still as hard as nails.

Sally: I just didn't want to sleep with you, so you had to write it off as a character flaw instead of dealing with the possibility that it might have something to do with you.

Harry: What's the statute of limitations on apologies?

Sally: Ten years.

Harry: Ooh. I can just get in under the wire.

(Clip 5B)

Sally: Would you like to have dinner with me sometime?

Harry: Are we becoming friends now?

Sally: Well, yeah.

Harry: Great. A woman friend. You know, you may be the first attractive woman I've not wanted to sleep with in my entire life.

Sally: That's wonderful, Harry.

Scene 6 Harry & Sally on the Phone—watching *Casablanca*

Scene Description: Harry and Sally are talking on the phone as the camera shows a variety of their activities, both alone and together. The scene ends with them talking on the phone in their separate beds as they watch Casablanca.

There are two voices: Sally and Harry

Sally: Hello.

Harry: You sleeping?

Sally: No, I was watching *Casablanc*a.

Harry: Channel, please.

Sally: Eleven.

Harry: Thank you. Got it.

(Clip 6A)

Harry: Now, you're telling me you would be happier with Victor Laslo than with Humphrey Bogart?

Sally: When did I say that?

Harry: When we drove to New York.

Sally: I never said that. I would never have said that.

Harry: All right, fine. Have it your way.

(End of Clip 6A)

Harry: Have you been sleeping?

Sally: Why?

Harry: 'Cause I haven't been sleeping.

I really miss Helen. Maybe I coming down with something. Last night I was up at four in the morning watching "Leave It to Beaver" in Spanish.

"Buenos días. Señora Cleaver. Dónde están Wallace y Theodore?"

I'm not well.

Sally: Well, I went to bed at seven-thirty last night. I haven't done that since the third grade.

Harry: Well, that's the good thing about depression. You get your rest.

Sally: I'm not depressed.

Harry: Okay, fine.

Do you still sleep on the same side of the bed?

Sally: I did for a while, but now I'm pretty much using the whole bed.

Harry: God, that's great. I feel weird when just my leg wanders over.

I miss her.

Sally: I don't miss him. I really don't.

Harry: Not even a little.

Sally: You know what I miss? I miss the idea of him.

Harry: Maybe I only miss the idea of her. No, I miss the whole Helen.

Sally: Last scene.

(Clip 6B)

Harry: Ingrid Bergman. Now she's low maintenance.

Sally: Low maintenance?

Harry: There are two kinds of women: high maintenance and low maintenance.

Sally   And Ingrid Bergman is low maintenance?

Harry: An L.M. Definitely.

Sally: Which one am I?

Harry: You're the worst kind. You're high maintenance, but you think you're low maintenance.

Sally: I don't see that.

Harry: You don't see that? "Waiter, I'll begin with the house salad, but I don't want the regular dressing. I'll have the balsamic vinegar and oil, but on the side, and then the salmon with the mustard sauce, but I want the mustard sauce on the side." "On the side" is a very big thing for you.

Sally: Well, I just want it the way I want it.

Harry: I know. High maintenance.

(End of Clip 6B)

Harry: Ooh. Best last line of a movie, ever.

I'm definitely coming down with something. Probably a twenty-four-hour tumor. They're going around.

Sally: You don't have a tumor.

Harry: How do you know?

Sally: If you're so worried, go see a doctor.

Harry: No, he'll just tell me it's nothing.

Sally: Will you be able to sleep?

Harry: If not, I'll be okay.

Sally: What'll you do?

Harry: I'll stay up and moan. Maybe I should practice now.

Sally: Good night, Harry.

Harry: Good night.